Alastor

By Maya Soni

Alastor
Copyright © 2022 by Maya Soni

All rights reserved. No part of this publication may be reproduced, distributed, or transmitted in any form or by any means, including photocopying, recording, or other electronic or mechanical methods, without the prior written permission of the author, except in the case of brief quotations embodied in critical reviews and certain other non-commercial uses permitted by copyright law.

Tellwell Talent
www.tellwell.ca

ISBN
978-0-2288-8356-2 (Paperback)

Dedicated to anyone who is struggling

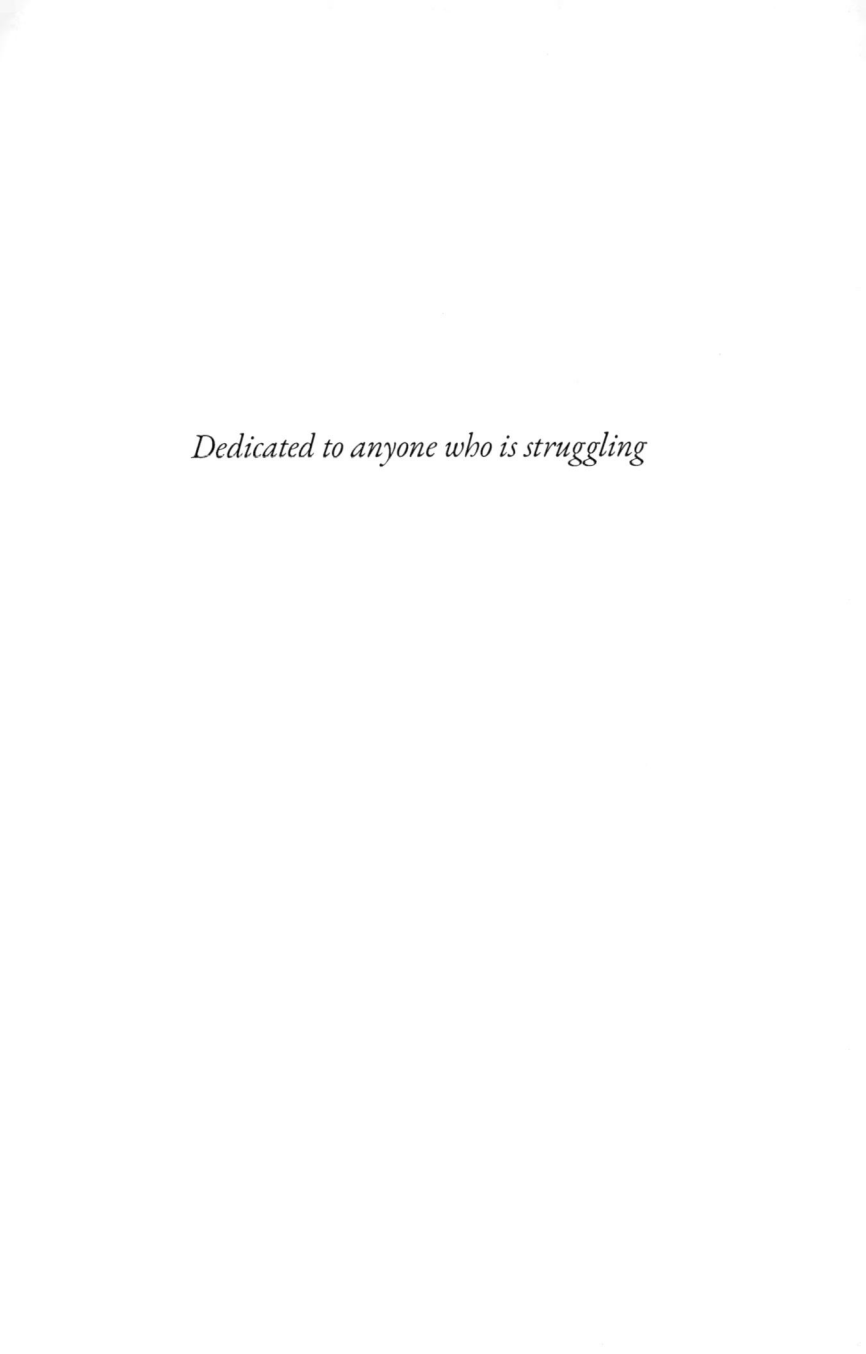

MESSAGE FROM THE AUTHOR

I wrote this book at the age of 14, now 15. I wrote just to write; there was no real purpose to it. But as I continued to write, I realized my anxiety was a big topic, so I decided that I was going to write a book about it. I never would have thought about publishing it, but I realized that this could help people. Help people not feel alone. This book is filled with my random, messy thoughts, my strong opinions, stupid humour, and emotions. This book is hopefully a good guide for those who don't understand anxiety and something relatable for those who do. I want this to be read like you're in my head and in my life. It's supposed to be chaotic and dramatic - just like me. Even if you don't deal with anxiety, maybe you can relate to the struggles of being a teenager. Anxiety is a big part of my life, it's a learning experience for me, too. I'm beyond grateful I had writing as an outlet for my anxiety and to be able to publish this. I would also like to put out a little warning, I do touch on some heavy subjects that might be sensitive for some people. So for those, be mindful while reading. Now I can introduce you to Alastor.

-Maya

CHAPTER ONE
nice to meet you

I t's Wednesday, December 8th, 2021, 7:41 in the morning. I'm on the bus to go to school and I'm tired. I'm getting anxious because I'm scared to see what the day will bring. I'm listening to soft music, but it isn't helping. Sometimes, even music gives me panic attacks and makes me sad or extra tired. But lately, I've just been on the edge, which isn't my favorite place to be. The bus is pulling up to the school, and I say thanks to the bus driver. I wish I knew his name; it makes me feel bad that I don't know it.

My Art and Tech Ed teachers are always at the door to spray our hands with sanitizer, and they always spray way too much. They give you enough for six hands. I walk upstairs quickly to class every day. I don't know why because I'm not eager to get to class, but it almost feels like a competition even though no one else is there.

I always get scared when I get to my locker because sometimes I can't open it, and it makes me feel like a big idiot and I feel like the other kids will judge me. I know they won't. It's just the way that I think, and I can't stop thinking like this for the life of me. I hate it. I'm normally one of the first in class, along with a couple of people I know and two of the quiet kids. It's awkward though because the people I know, who I'm kind of friends with, leave to see friends outside of class and I just sit there in silence with the quiet kids - it makes me uncomfortable. Eventually, my two best friends, Ila & Morgan, get here. Ila is tall and has short blonde hair with blue eyes. Morgan is a little shorter than Ila with long dark brown hair & hazel eyes. I talk to them, and my gloominess goes away. I feel the need to be okay in front of them or just okay in general. Not that it would be weird or whatever it's just not something that needs to happen or to be worried about.

Ila and Morgan are my friends, and I love them, but socializing with them even for ten minutes in the morning makes me tired. My 'social battery' as people like to call it runs out quickly and usually it's from being social or talking. I put my head down in most classes or just pretend that I'm paying attention because my brain is so run down that it can't retain or comprehend any of the information that's being thrown at me. But that's when I get worried. Like if there's a test or a quiz on this, and I can't remember any of it or can't do it, it stresses me out. School is one of the top ten things that I hate.

School is over, and every afternoon on the bus I blast my music on my AirPods to try to drown out the voices of the annoying, obnoxious kids on my bus who just never know when to shut up. It's relieving to get off the bus. At home, I say hi to the kids my mom takes care of, say hi to my mom, and the animals; Joey and Twinkie, our cats, and Copper, our dog.

Since I don't eat at school or barely eat at school, I stuff my face and pig out on whatever food we have at home and then feel guilty afterward. Why do we feel that guilt, though? What made us think that we have to feel guilty for eating a lot after starving ourselves all day? Either way, I just say that I always make up for what I didn't eat during the school day at home.

In my room, I just sit on my bed and go on my phone. I'm too exhausted to do any homework at this point, so I leave it for later. It may sound like I procrastinate, but I don't. That's one thing my anxiety is good for. It makes sure I get every single thing done even if I don't have to, like homework or cleaning or laundry. I feel obligated to do these things. But normally, my room is already clean because when I feel anxious or stressed, I clean. It's kind of a coping mechanism. Sometimes, I wish there were more things for me to clean or more laundry for me to do.

And oddly, I get extremely anxious or overwhelmed for no reason, and I feel like I need to scream or something. And when I feel like that, I imagine myself running up my street in the cold, with the wind hitting my face with so much aggression, and I would run into the woods (avoiding the tree branches jutting out). And in these woods, there would be this little hill or mountain, but it's small, like the size of a car. But I see myself standing on this hill and just screaming my heart out, and I would think I might start to cry, but I don't. It's all anger and exhaustion. But that doesn't surprise me, to be honest, because sometimes I find it hard to cry.

I also don't like to look in the mirror without any makeup on. It's kind of depressing. All I see are big dark circles and a pale, run-down looking face. When I wear makeup, I keep it pretty natural, but there's just enough to cover up the imperfections. I never used to be so insecure. I was confident for so long, and then something just changed, and I hated everything about myself.

Like, I don't feel like I'm as skinny as I should be, or have a sharp enough jawline, not enough freckles, my hair is too frizzy, my nose is ugly, or my eye bags make me look unwell. Sadly, there are a lot more things I don't like about myself. It's really hard to try to be something and someone who you don't want to be. But I guess I'll tell you what I look like, so you can get to know me better. I'm average height for my age, maybe 5'4". I'm tinier than I feel. Underweight for being 14. I have brown hair not too far past my collarbone. And brown eyes with some freckles sprinkled across my face. I feel like people around me think I don't care about how I look. But that's not true at all, I take everything into consideration. I care so much about how I look, especially my outfit. I think about how people will view me and what *other* people will think. I wear sweatpants and hoodies mostly, I don't like tight clothes. Except for leggings. I make sure my hair looks good, not greasy. If I have a pimple I'll cover that up real good. Do everything I can to look okay. I used to have super long hair, all the way down to my waist. I liked it when it was long, some people liked it too, some people hated it. It was a lot to take care of though, it was hard to work with long hair. Last March I chopped 8 inches off. That's a lot of hair. I donated it though, so it will get used. It was a big change for me but I really needed it. I needed something different. I'm not sure if I like it short or long better, I just know it's *way* easier to take care of my hair now. A lot of people cut or dye their hair when they are going through a mental breakdown but I didn't cut my hair because I was going through one. I don't want to be too impulsive. But I just think I needed to change. Anyways my insecurities have made me someone that I don't even want to be around because I don't know who she is. She isn't me and she isn't who I used to be. I miss the old me; she was always so content and did whatever she wanted, anything that she loved and enjoyed. And she didn't care about anything people said to/about her. She brushed it off and forgot about it the next day. She was bright and creative, and that made her smart. She wasn't tired all the time or constantly worried about everything. She was happy. I think society and social media did a lot of the damage, but the friends I had did some of the harm, too. Friends can be great unless they're toxic and belittle you. Ila and Morgan are the complete opposite; they are the best friends I've ever had. They make me feel better.

And even though I have really bad anxiety, when there's a controversial problem or debate, my anxiety is completely gone. Don't get me wrong, it haunts me later, but I get heated and argumentative in the moment, and I enjoy it.

There are way too many things that I could argue about, like the education system, sexism, discrimination, mental health, human rights, society, and so much more. But the toxicity of my debating trait is that no matter what, I think I'm right; and I am. If I wasn't 100% sure that I was right, I wouldn't interfere unless it's a circumstantial problem. Like we always get into debates in health. Because a lot of those topics have to do with health.

I'm a very opinionated person and I think that it's good because no one can change my mind. I'm very stubborn and determined which is good, and bad for me. I would like to say that I'm pretty persuasive and a bit manipulative, but normally it's all for the best of things. You may think that I'm a good decision maker from this but I'm the total opposite and it's my anxiety's fault.

I'm indecisive. I don't make very many decisions for myself unless I have, like I said, a strong opinion about it. After my debater self is done feuding, my anxiety likes to haunt me with it all. Like saying "omg that was so embarrassing for you, you got all heated for nothing! It was just a debate." Or "what if you're wrong? I know that it's scientifically proven to be right, but what if you're wrong?" But my favorite is "why did you say that?!" and "why did you say it like that?!" or "Omg you like to make a fool of yourself, don't you?" Yeah, that one gets me the most.

Right now I'm thinking of naming my anxiety, giving it a name. Because it's kind of like a friend that you secretly hate but they're the only friend you have so you can't say anything. That's what my anxiety is like, except it knows I hate it but just doesn't want to leave.

Another annoying thing is how draining anxiety can be. I'm constantly tired all the time. And it's not fun. I wake up and go to bed tired. It feels like I've done so much when I've done absolutely nothing. I don't understand how & why anxiety can make you tired, I don't understand a lot of it. But I have to deal with it either way. Sometimes I feel so tired I just wanna cry & sleep at the same time because I'm so stressed but I don't know what I'm stressed about because there isn't much for me to worry about. Normally at school, I can manage the tiredness just enough to seem okay but sometimes I can't manage it and I have to put my head down or go to the washroom to wake myself up. That's when people start to ask if I'm okay. And I know Ila and Morgan care when they ask but I can't see how anyone else could care. They probably think there's drama and just want to know what happened. But either way, I don't like it when people ask if I'm okay. It almost gets me more in a slump.

People often make fun of my sleep schedule. I go to bed at 8:30 and wake up at 6:00. That's a lot of sleep for a 14-year-old. Too much sleep. But I feel like I never get enough sleep. I always need more or I need strong coffee or caffeinated tea to keep me awake. Yet another thing that I don't understand. *I think* that part of the reason is that I'm not physically tired, I'm mentally tired, and there's a big difference. Except mental exhaustion can give you physical symptoms which sucks. I'm sore, achy, & dizzy all the time. My eyes are heavy, I have headaches, I'm almost slow in a way like a sloth, and I feel weak and ill. I wouldn't say I'm moody but I can get annoyed a little easier, and I feel down.

Okay - I have finally decided what to name my anxiety or my mental illness. It's between Abaddon which means angel of death in Hebrew, or Alastor which means tormentor or harasser in Ancient Greek. But I think I have to go with Alastor because it seems to be more fitting, and I can call him Al for short.

CHAPTER TWO
The basics

Al tortures me until I snap. He wears me down slowly, then all at once he breaks me. He fills my head with awful thoughts, thoughts that scare me, enrage me, and thoughts that make me depressed. I am miserable. I dread waking up because of the intruding thoughts, and I look forward to going to sleep to put them to rest. Day in and day out, *I never stop thinking.* I wish often for my head, or Al, to just ***shut up.*** It's overwhelming all these opinions, horrible words, offensive things, just being tossed around in my head 24 hours a day, seven days a week. It's stressful.

Anxiety is starting to feel like a disease spreading all around my head, my chest, my stomach, and soon all over my body. I'm infected and it's taking over. The last thing I want is for it to start controlling me, even more than it does now. I first started taking medication in late springtime of 2021; 25 mg of Sertraline Zoloft. Then I moved to 50mg then 75mg then 100mg then to 125mg which is what I'm at now but it's still not working. A week or two ago I started 1 mg of Aripiprazole so it's too early to see if it will do me any good yet. But I'm hoping that this change will be the one to make me better. I think all the meds improved my mood a bit but nothing about my anxiety changed. If anything, it's gotten worse over the last few months. I have many different physical symptoms of anxiety that you would never know are from anxiety. Like how I'm so tired all the time. I'm shaky a lot in my hands or legs, or there is this horrible knot in my stomach when I'm anxious and *I **hate** it* and there's nothing I can do to get rid of it.

I feel a lot of guilt about my anxiety and my mental state, just because I react the way I do to it and I complain about it all the time when there are so many people out there going through things 10x worse than me. And I always try to tell myself that I have it good, everything is okay there's no reason to feel the way I do, you don't have any right to feel that way.

And that sounds harsh to say but it's true, isn't it? And this also makes me feel like a wimp because of all the people who have it rough and I'm the way I am, acting the way I do.

There is one thing I can't believe I forgot to mention, maybe because it feels so normal now. But it's covid time and I live in Nova Scotia. It normally isn't too bad here but recently it's been getting kind of scary. I never knew anyone with covid, it kinda seems like since I wear my mask and wash my hands and do everything I'm supposed to, I won't get it and my friends won't either. But Morgan tested positive on a rapid test so technically I'm a close contact. Which is scary. She got a PCR test and we're waiting for the results and I swear to god if it's a positive I'm gonna flip out. Covid could have hit me at any time and it decided to hit me now, at the worst time possible. It's Christmas time and I want to be able to spend it with my family. Also, I get my braces in three days, the only thing I've been looking forward to for months. It sounds strange that I'm excited to get braces but it's true and if I can't get them I'll probably cry. I got my PCR today at 4:40 so I'm just hoping that it comes back negative.

If I do get covid my anxiety will be through the roof and I will probably get depressed because of being in isolation and all the things I was excited about and looking forward to being canceled because you caught a virus, you'd be depressed too. I will probably be the happiest person alive if my test comes back negative. My fingers are crossed.

The nervousness I have in anticipation of the test is crazy. There are knots in my stomach and they're getting tighter and tighter. I keep thinking about if I do get it and I do have covid, how will I handle it? Physically I think I'll be fine, just a rough cold. But mentally? I'll be a wreck.

Morgan, with whom I was a close contact, tested positive on her PCR. I was terrified. My stomach had knots for two days straight. I went to get my PCR test done on Saturday, the 18th, and got the results the next day. I am negative. Thank God. I didn't know what to do with myself while waiting for my results. I was doing everything and anything to keep myself busy. But I'm just happy that I can get my braces, leave the house, spend Christmas with my family, and not have to be stuck in the house anymore. But I feel absolutely horrible

Alastor

for her. I couldn't even imagine what it would be like in her situation. Covid is scary and it's stressful. But, since my mind works the way it does I still think there's a way that I won't get my braces or Christmas isn't going to happen the way it should. I hate that Al has to try to ruin everything. But something he can't ruin. Something that's fully mine. It's my family. My family means so much to me, and sometimes I feel guilty because I don't show them how much they mean to me. They go above and beyond for me and I don't know why. My dad cares so much for me and does everything he can for me, he's the most selfless person I know and insanely generous. My dad is tall and has a dark tan to his skin. He is always on the go, doing something new. And he also has a very bad humor, lots of dad jokes.

My mum is such a sympathetic person and knows how to make you feel better when you're down, (she helps me with my anxiety a lot) She is short and has gray thick hair with glasses. She is very peppy and pretty nifty. My brother is my brother. We fight a lot because we're siblings but I know he cares, it shows but he tries to hide it. He's the comedic relief in the house. He is pretty tall, very slim and has dark brown hair that's almost black. He puts up a serious 'I'm too cool' front a lot. But in reality he is super goofy. I could never forget the animals, Joey the oldest is a chubby cat and the sweetest sleeper. Joey doesn't like too much affection but he's such a good dude. Copper, the second oldest, is our quirky little dog with an underbite, he's the cutest cuddler and a sidekick to our mom. I think we don't appreciate him as much as we should. Lastly Twinkie, my youngest sibling is a feisty & sassy black cat and my best friend. She has always been there for me and immediately clicked with me. She is misunderstood, people think she is a mean cat but she really isn't. She clearly just doesn't like you.

I don't know what I would do without my family, I'm so grateful for every single one of them. I am not me without my family. I couldn't live without them. I'm thankful that I feel comfortable to talk to my parents about my anxiety and to open up to them. My parents are my best friends, I tell them pretty much everything. My brother not so much, he's not the easiest to talk to, mostly just because we are siblings. But I feel so bad for him sometimes, because he has it rough. He's not the best in school or good at cleaning up after himself or

Alastor

taking care of himself. My parents don't expect much from us besides our best, they just want us to do our best. But it's hard for him because I think we get compared to each other a lot. You can't do that with us though because we are *complete* opposites. We think, do, act differently. Nothing to compare. To be honest I'm not entirely sure why I feel so bad for him, I guess there isn't a specific reason. Things just seem hard for him, he has to deal with a lot so young.

And my parents understand that. They let me stay home if I need to, they don't have high expectations for us, they are beyond caring and probably the best parents you could ever ask for.

I include Ila & Morgan as family because school and life in general wouldn't be the same without them. Ila is such a bubbly person who makes your day a little brighter and inspirers, and Morgan is such a loyal comforting friend who, without trying, makes you laugh. School would be unbearable without you guys. Both of them are super smart. Ila is definitely more silly, but can be serious when needed too. Morgan is a lot more studious, not so serious but calmer.

But she definitely has a silly side though. And for me, as a friend im definitely a lot more silly, stupid, and weird most of the time im with them. But I'm always trying to make them laugh. I love making them laugh. But me and Morgan have similar personalities. We have social anxieties in common and are mostly quiet in public. When it's just the three of us though, Ila and I are more alike. Like Dumb and Dumber, im Dumber. We entertain Morgan.

But besides my family I love a lot of other things. Like coffee, tea, my bed, my giant stuffed emotional support bear that I named Cornelius Jr., other random things like Criminal Minds, Marvel, Taylor Swift songs or music in general, sweatpants & hoodies, pasta, kale chips. There's probably 100 other things too. Another thing I love is running. Especially when I'm sad, because it feels like I'm running away from something. I'm most likely trying to run away from my problems but who doesn't try to do that. I use running as a way to cope, and it's super helpful.

I also like movies and tv shows so much because it kind of feels like a way to not be where I am. So like I'm in a world with superheroes who can save me when I need it. I like watching tv a lot because it feels like a way to get away or a place to escape to. Kind of the same thing with music. It doesn't take me somewhere else but it helps me focus on something else.

Music distracts me in a good way. One more thing that I love is doing makeup. No matter if it's *pretty* makeup or special effects makeup, I find it really fun. I wouldn't say I use it to express myself but I use it as an outlet to cope. Even though I'm not *really* coping I just distract myself by keeping busy. I've gotten kind of good at it since I've been doing it for over a year.

There are a ton of things that I'd love to do. I want to do so much traveling, I have a list of places that I'd like to visit. I want to go cliff jumping and bridge jumping. I want to go to more concerts, meet celebrities, drive a car, and make money. But I'm afraid my anxiety will prevent me from it. It won't let me take risks.

I want to go to university and study criminology & psychology so I can do something in that field because it really interests me. But I don't know if Al will let me get there, or maybe he will let me get there but just tear me apart on the way. I want to be successful and not have money troubles. But mostly I just want to be happy.

Right now everyone tells me that my anxiety isn't going to last forever & that it will go away, but it feels like it's the only thing that's gonna last. It feels like it's always going to be there and it's never going to leave, it's going to be something that I'll always have to deal with. Something I'm going to take to the grave.

I hope I'm not like all of those people who become their mental illnesses. It seems pathetic to me, but it's inevitable for people who struggle with it. They can't help it. I don't want to have anxiety forever. I don't want to have it at all. But there's nothing I can do about it. I don't want my anxiety to eat me up and ruin me. I want to get better.

CHAPTER THREE
Panic attacks

Society has probably ruined my life and will continue to ruin my life unless I can learn how to not let it bother me. And that seems hard. I think that society has been controlling me since the 6th grade. When I started to care about my looks, clothes, what I have, what I *don't* have, how smart I am, how athletic I am, or who my friends are. Social media is a big part of society. Making everyone feel insecure or like they need something because their friends or a celebrity has it. Like if they get that product they'll turn pretty.

Or it will make you feel left out, seeing people who are your '*friends'* hangout without you. That one has definitely happened to me the most. Anyway, society sucks. Making you think you have to look, act, be or have certain things. And if you don't you're weird and not cool. Doesn't it sound stupid?

I'm also not sure if my anxiety makes me think this way or it's my insecurities or maybe even both. But I constantly think that people think I'm annoying or weird. Or that I'm in their way, I'm an inconvenience. That's how I think people see me. They don't want to be around me, or try to avoid me at all costs. So sometimes I question why Morgan & Ila hang out with me. They could ditch me at any point, but they don't. And they reassure me and tell me that they wouldn't hang out with me if they didn't like me. Which might sound a little funny but if you think about it, it's nice. Because they hangout with me every day, and talk to me all the time. They check in on me when they can tell I'm down. I don't think I show my appreciation to them as much as I should.

Sometimes I find it hard to explain what panic attacks are like. It's hard for Ila and Morgan to understand since they've never had one. I'm going to try now. Most of the time I can feel them when they're coming, I don't know when they'll come or have a time frame. It would be nice so I can prepare, but it's not that easy. My stomach is in knots and I feel on edge, my breathing feels off, and it feels like something bad is going to happen. Something really bad, as I freak out silently.

Alastor

First my legs start to tap and my hands start to shake and I start to fidget. Then my breathing gets really fast, almost feels like I can't breathe or catch my breath. Normally I start to cry, my eyes start to water and the tears won't stop. During this, in my head it feels like nothing and everything is happening. My head is so overwhelmed and hectic but nothing is happening. It's a blur. I'm scared, and I'm confused because I don't know what I'm scared of. Once I reach this point there isn't a way to get back to the normalcy I had to begin with. It takes me a long time to calm down, I kind of have to just deal with it until it passes. After I've calmed down a bit I'm still on edge for the majority of the day, but I'm also exhausted. All the panic attacks I can remember having I've always fallen asleep not long after, because it completely drains me. Once I sleep a bit I feel a bit better for the rest of the day, but I also feel completely embarrassed. For what reason I don't know, because it's not something I can control but it makes me feel weak in a way, fragile. And *I hate that*. I don't want to be seen as weak, I want to be seen as strong, but I feel the absolute opposite.

CHAPTER FOUR
Getting older

I'm getting so tired and so sick of Al. He is so annoying, he nags at me and bugs me. He seriously has nothing else to do? Even on Christmas, he takes no days off. Besides Al being a pain, my Christmas was good and my winter break hasn't been bad either. I'm not looking forward to school starting up again because I'm feeling extra exhausted lately and school on top of that won't be nice.

One of the biggest reasons I hate going to school is because I feel scared and vulnerable there. Like I can be attacked at any given point. When I'm at home in my room I feel safe and protected. I'm also a home body so I like being home rather than being out. I don't know what it is but school gives me this horrible feeling that makes me want to turn around and walk home. Walk the 3 hour walk home. And most people would think something happened at school that traumatized me to make me not want to go, but there's nothing significant that I can remember. To be honest, I feel like it traumatizes me a little bit everyday and everyday I've gone. But it still doesn't make sense to me. Doesn't make sense for what causes the unwelcome feeling I get.

The whole environment of school sucks, almost all my teachers suck, the kids are rude and judgmental. There's no place that you're comfortable. It feels like *everyone* is watching and judging you. And you try not to care but you end up caring even more. Because in school, especially at this age, you can't do *anything* wrong according to the social norms or you're considered weird. Not normal.

Speaking of school we have been mostly going in person during covid, except for about a month last year we went online. At first I thought it was great because there was no way that I could get anxious right? I proved that point wrong. I was in English class and we were doing attendance, normally the teachers were ok when students had their camera off and just typed in the chat box that they were there. So that's what I was doing but my teacher never saw that I was there apparently and kept pushing me to turn my microphone and camera on. My fingers were shaking as I was trembling to write in the chat box that my mic and camera are broken, which they are not. I just wasn't comfortable having either of them on. As I was hitting send both Ila and Morgan were messaging my phone telling me to turn it on. At that point I couldn't breathe and my heart was beating so fast. Tears started forming in my eyes and rolling down my face. I was freaking out. All I could think of doing was getting out, getting out of the situation I was in. So I shut the laptop and sat in my bed for a second contemplating what to do. That experience has traumatized me. It might not happen again and it probably won't, but it scares me so much that there's a chance it *might*.

We have online school for a week, 5 days. Which I don't see why there's a point to even doing it for just 5 days but whatever. There's so many different things that can happen in 5 days that are bad. And from the way I think, it feels like all of them are going to happen to me. Which is scary. Before I have to deal with that, it's my birthday, January 8th, 2 days from now. I don't like my birthday very much. I haven't for a few years now. I don't like the thought that in 2 days I spent *years* wasted on being sad and anxious when I could've been living my life happily. And I blame it on myself first but then I realize it's Alastor I have to blame. He is so hard on me, and I just want a break even just for a day. But he would never give that to me. I feel like in all the 15 years I've been on this planet, I haven't done anything. Nothing memorable. Feels like a waste. I just wasted a *soon to be* 15 years and that scares me. Makes it seem like I'm running out of time. I'm running out of time to get rid of Alastor and to have the chance to be genuinely happy so I can live a good life. Many people would say that sounds stupid because I'm only a teenager, but it doesn't feel stupid. It's a genuine fear, running out of time. Running out of time being a kid before you have to grow up and go to college. Running out of time in college before you have to get a job and get a life. Then you run out of time *having* a life. A bit dramatic but that's the way I am.

It was my birthday yesterday, the night before I was dreading waking up. Hoping I could stop time for this one night. I felt off when I woke up being 15 I was almost depressed in a way, disappointed. I was anxious even though I was already 15 but

I was anxious and felt something bad was going to happen. I could tell my parents knew I was off and they were trying to make me feel better. It was kind of obvious they were offering me things and being extra nice. Maybe it was because it was *my birthday* but it didn't feel like that. I'm really grateful for that and all but it didn't help, it's hard for it to get better without a big distraction. So when my friends got here it was better, I kind of *had* to be better. But besides being stressed out while they were here I had a lot of fun. I have good friends so it's not hard to have fun.

Something else I find really scary is the life most adults live nowadays. School, university, job, marriage, more jobs, kids, more jobs, retirement, old age, death. People say life is the little things, the good stuff. But to *me* I don't see people living like that happy. Working jobs just so they have money to pay the bills. Living in a home suitable for their children who are definitely annoying. And fighting with your husband over I don't even know what. I don't see 'happy' anywhere in there. I know a lot of things I want that I can't change because of laws or whatever but I want to work a job that makes me happy and live somewhere that makes me happy. I don't want to be stressed over bills and buying groceries. I don't want the days to be repeating, I want some spontaneity. I want life to be something worth living. I want to be the person who enjoys life and the person who lives in the moment. I know that I'm the total opposite of that right now, but that's what I *want* to be. I can also understand that people close to me have to go through a lot because of my anxiety, not just family but everyone. I feel bad about it because it's really hard for me to try to explain what's going on, and it's really hard for them to understand because they can't read my mind. So sometimes they will say things or do things that I already know. I already get beaten up by Alastor about the things I say and do, and the way I deal with things. So when other people say the same stuff he's already said, it's frustrating because I hear it enough. But obviously I know that it's not their fault because they can't read my mind but it makes me so angry and I'm not sure why. All I hear in my head when people say things is "don't you think I already know that? Don't you think I already know that? Don't you think I already know that?" All. I. Hear. It feels like I'm being targeted not only by Alastor but now by the people around me. Again I know they don't know and it's not their fault, it's Alastor's.

Alastor

January is almost over which means it's February soon which means it's Valentine's Day. I like Valentine's Day mostly because of the stuffed animals and chocolate. I personally think I'm too young to have a boyfriend quite yet, maybe in high school but not now. Also with everything going on with me I don't think a boyfriend would be good right now. I honestly make fun of everyone who is dating right now because they are so awkward and I find it hilarious. No offense to them, but middle school relationships don't normally last. They last like a week or a month if you're lucky and they end in the most dramatic ways. It's very entertaining. Even though I don't celebrate Valentine's the regular way, my friends and I are doing a Galentine's day. We will watch a movie, eat chocolate and buy ourselves valentine stuffed animals. I think it will be fun.

Oh also I remember telling you about getting my braces on but I can't remember if I told you that I got them. I'm still really happy about them, I got a color and it's purple. I don't mind them, they didn't hurt at all either which is good. I get my bottom ones on in three days and bottoms are supposed to hurt more, so I wouldn't be surprised if I'm in a little discomfort. -I got them and they hurt.

CHAPTER FIVE
A New Year

Since it's the beginning of 2022, I thought I should tell you a few things. I had a pretty rough year but there were definitely some really good moments. I'm hoping that 2022 will have even more happy moments and less bad moments. I have some goals too: drink less coffee, more water, workout more, make healthier snacks, write more in this book, and lastly fill any free time doing a hobby or something productive. Rather than going on my phone. Social media and phones, every teenage kid has a phone. I go on my phone a lot. Whenever I'm bored, or anxious, or uncomfortable. I mostly go on it when I'm bored though. Because I don't feel like getting up and doing anything. I'd prefer to lay on my bed and just entertain myself with social media which is probably the worst thing to do because social media is so bad for you. I have absolutely no motivation to do anything productive or anything for enjoyment. I'm just so tired. Too tired to do anything. I go on my phone when I'm anxious, mostly to distract myself. Try to block or hide away all the thoughts and feelings. When I spend time on my phone I feel guilty and Unproductive. Feels like I'm wasting my time. Which I am. I could be doing 100 other things that would be more beneficial for me. My parents get annoyed that I'm on my phone so much and I feel bad because I could be spending that time with them but I'm not. It's hard to try to explain why I'm on it all the time because it probably just seems like I'm lazy. But not much I can do about it. Phones can be good for a lot of things. But most things it's good for, I don't need or use. Just contacting my friends, learning, help, or entertainment. Phones got everyone in a choke hold. A hold that feels like protection, but really isn't.

Side tracked, sorry- I'm hoping I left all my toxicity in 2021 and 2022 will be a better year for me. 2021 did give me some good things. I got closer with my friend Charlotte & me and my friend Ella are now really good friends. We absorbed Ella into our trio of me, Ila and morgan. Ella is sporty blonde with medium long blonde hair & hazel eyes. Ella is really funny and she makes me laugh a lot. When in public she is chill with a dry humor, but when just the four of us she is just as goofed up like the rest of us. And I've been friends with Charlotte for quite awhile now, about 4 years. She is short, well a little shorter than me. And she has long light brown hair with brown eyes. She's quiet, & super chill, she's always someone you can talk to.

Anyways I'm now getting the help that I need, I take care of myself more (physically definitely not mentally) but still baby steps right? I also found more things that I like doing like cooking and makeup. 2021 did do harm but it also gave me things that I'm grateful for. Fingers crossed that 2022 will be a good year. I like to surround myself with positive people, people who don't fuel the negativity. If they do, I try really hard to not let it get to me. I want to feel happy around the people I'm with and right now I mostly am. I got rid of all the toxic friends I had a long time ago, and I don't miss them one bit. They were bad for me. I see them in the halls at school and I wonder to myself, "Who are they making miserable now?" Normally what gets me the most is that they are so passive aggressive and it's so annoying. Sometimes I feel bad for them, that they have such sad lives so they need to be rude to others. Most of the people I was friends with that were toxic, weren't always toxic. They were quiet, and scared to speak their minds, they seemed vulnerable. Now they are stuck up and conceded, and don't care about other people's feelings. That's why I stopped being friends with them. Because on top of Alastor, I don't need to deal with them.

My friends definitely were a big part of what got me through the year. I don't think I'd be well and able if I didn't have them. They keep me distracted in a way. Help me not think all the time. By hanging out after school and on the weekends, or just making me laugh in class. Music and tv were also a big factor. I love music so listening to music always helps, tv doesn't distract me too much but it still helps though. Even though I've only been writing to you for a month this year, it definitely helped me end my year off better. You have been an outlet for me, so thank you. My parents being so helpful definitely helps, same with my aunt, she is always trying to help. Which is nice. My animals also being there for me is good too. Lysol disinfectant cleaner was also nice to have with me this year. Helped me cope when I was stressed.

Alastor

I think getting adaptations for school was also good, how I got them is not my favorite story, but I got them. Adaptations are when the school does things or exempts you from things to make it easier for you. It's Comforting to know that they're there. Ms C & Ms G being such good teachers is also amazing. I feel comfortable in their classes. They are every student's favorite teacher. They actually care about their students and want to teach us. They make us look forward to going to class because they create an environment where we enjoy learning & enjoy being there. I'm very different in their class compared to other classes. Because they make you feel like you're in a safe place. I don't think many teachers understand that in order for your students to want to respect you, you have to respect them. Because it goes both ways. Ms G & Ms C get that. Some of the other teachers are good too, and other teachers not so much but I'm just thankful I at least have two really good ones.

CHAPTER SIX
School nights

I don't think I've ever told you about when I first came to middle school. That was one bad day. I came to middle school with a huge friend group. Even though I had such a big friend group, I didn't have a best friend. Anyways on our first day half the friend group was gone, because they knew some of the kids there from sports or family. Then maybe two weeks to a month later more of the friend group was gone because they had made new friends. So to sum that up middle school ate and devoured our friend group and left the scraps. And I was one of them. Everyone envied one table of kids. People would probably label them as the 'cool kids' because yes, those are real. I'm not sure why everyone likes them so much because they're rude and say mean things and call it a joke while laughing. I think the reason I might sound jealous or envious is because a lot of the kids in that friend group I grew up with. I've known them & have been friends with them since grade 1 and as soon as we come to middle school we're not friends anymore. I get it though, everyone loses and gains friends in middle school, it's normal. I still talk to some of them here and there, we're friendly. But that's it.

Middle school is where I met Morgan though. Morgan and I had a mutual friend. We both had our own tiny friend groups, 'trios' and for any project or partner work we'd get left out. So two out of our trio would get together and we'd be lonely, so we started to become partners for any of that work. And we weren't close but we were friends. So in grade 8 we ended up being in the same class again, and then Ila was in our class. I met Ila wayyy before grade 8. I was actually best friends with Ila way back in elementary school, but she moved away for a few years because of her dad's job, then came back. At first, the three of us weren't really friends, we were just nice to each other. But Ila and I became closer and absorbed Morgan into our friendship. So we were a trio, and we made sure no one gets left out or feels left out. Which is important to us. So now in grade 9 we are still all best friends and Ila was in my class for two years and Morgan was in my class my whole time at middle school. Which is nice to think about, because even though we weren't friends for all of it, they were always there.

This week was our first week back in person at school. All I try to think of is that it could've gone worse. It was easy because my friends were there but I just remember how tiring it is to just be there. How it drains you. It leaves you with a gross feeling. And I don't know what it was but this week I felt extra paranoid, like everyone was staring at me 24/7. Like something was wrong with the way I looked or I said something. Also this week Ila wasn't there because she got covid, most likely from sports. So now, both Morgan and Ila have had covid, and I think it's just a matter of time before I get it. I've been beyond lucky. I think I'd enjoy quarantine though, I'd get to stay in my room all the time, eat food, watch tv, read, do makeup, go on my phone, clean and organize everything twice, and no one can say anything about it. It would be heaven. I know Morgan enjoyed it too, because she is an introvert like me and we like that sort of stuff. But Ila isn't. She is definitely an extrovert and likes going out and doing things, she likes to be busy. So I feel bad because this is her worst nightmare. But Morgan also had to have covid during Christmas, so they both had/have it bad.

I have only been back *in* school for a week and a day and I'm completely exhausted, overwhelmed and just done with it in general. The workload isn't too much but just seems so heavy. I'm hoping it will get better, or to feel better at least. It is the first couple weeks back, so I might just be transitioning back into routine. Everything seems to be transitioning fine except for actually being *at* school. I also think that I could be stressed over what we're doing in school. We're picking high school courses and I'm completely unprepared and have no clue what any of the courses are. I also think that because we're talking about high school so much it's freaking me out a bit. Because it is a whole different place with completely different people and teachers, & they expect way more from you. It's a whole new territory. I'm just glad I have time to prepare myself. I've been acting funny recently and I think it's just because I'm on edge but in class I can't handle the noise. I normally can manage, it's annoying but I can manage. It was bothering me so much in one class and I just couldn't focus so I put my AirPods in and blasted my white noise that I use to sleep. I know that sounds funny, but it helped so who cares.

Also I've been saying that a lot lately. "Who cares", "I don't care". Which is good and bad for me. It helps with my anxiety. So if Alastor is saying things like "oh they're probably talking about you, about the way you look, sound, or the way you do things." And I just don't really care anymore, I'm gonna do what I *want* to do or what I *can* do. Which might sound good but it's not, because it gets like this sometimes. It happens when I'm burnt out. I start slacking hard, getting lazy & depressed. My grades drop, I don't leave the house. I managed to not fail but my math grade for example went from a 69 to 67 then to a 61.

Like I said, I don't fail but I don't do good. Math isn't my best grade, never my highest, always my lowest. I've always needed help in math. But my mark has been extra low lately. Because of the "I don't care" mentality things are rough, but what can you do?

Normally the days always feel like repeating but when I'm like this, it's worse. It feels like a continuous painful loop, over and over, the same day every day. I get ready for school; attempt to make bed, get dressed, wash my face, put makeup on, get stuff packed, eat, caffeinate, brush teeth, walk dog, leave for bus. After that when I'm at school I go to all my classes that bore me, maybe eat lunch maybe don't, feel judged, gross, & anxious. Then I get on the bus come home, eat, go on my phone, watch tv, get stuff ready for next day of school, go on my phone again & watch tv again, then get ready for bed, look if I have homework, (which normally I do but just don't do it). Then I take my meds, say goodnight to everyone, then sleep. I sleep for probably 9 hours and still wake up exhausted. I've tried different sleeping schedules, I did research, but *nothing* fixed me being tired all the time.

And that's it. All of that repeating over and over for about 300 days of the year. Living the life aren't I? I shouldn't say that though because some people would kill to live like I do. Why am I so ungrateful? In the future I don't want that. I want spontaneity. I want to take risks and for everyday to feel like a new day, a different day. I want to have a job I enjoy going to everyday, friends and family that make me happy. No financial troubles.

Speaking of jobs. Both my parents have ok jobs. I don't like my dad's job because he doesn't like it. He works at the hospital and he is a cook. His job does give him a ton of insurance for health & stuff so that's good, but it also takes stuff away, I don't know the business stuff of it, but whatever. That job literally drains him and it doesn't make him happy. I think that he is being the 'live to work' type when he should be the 'work to live' which is what I want to be. That job is just so negative and not healthy for him, but he is trying to transfer to a job he likes better, so I hope it works out.

My mom is an in-home daycare provider. So it's private child care. That may sound very business-like but it's not at all. We become family with the kids & the family of the kids that she takes care of. They are pretty much like my siblings, they are here 5 days a week from 7-5. But they get on my nerves a lot. Mostly because I'm so close to them and am home a lot.

They really are like my siblings. They like to follow me to my room and pick around my stuff which is funny, they love my room so much and I'm not sure why. They used to bug me more when I was younger because when they were little they messed up my stuff and the amount of things they broke in my room is crazy. There was *always* a crib in my room, or I wasn't able to go to my room because a kid was napping in there. And as a pre teen that's very frustrating. Your stuff, your room, your snacks, and your own mom, all being shared by 5 kids plus you. They still bug me a little now just cause if they're loud when I'm trying to focus or they ate the last of the chocolate chip cookies, or you had laundry folded and they threw it on the floor. I understand that they're young and don't know any better but it's just hard when it's in your *own* home. These things don't get to me much now but one thing that *will* annoy me a lot in the future is the cribs. It's been a really long time since a baby had to nap in my room and it wasn't fun. But soon it will happen again. They won't be in there for long which is okay, but their crib is still annoying taking up space, or I'll find a soother or a stuffy under my bed. And it just bugs me so much because I get one space in the house, 1, and it's being taken over by my mom's job. My parents' job shouldn't affect *my* space, because it's <u>*mine*</u>. I understand that it's my mom's job, how she pays the bills and pays for our stuff. It's just really annoying. Like I said it's not the kid's themselves it's the stuff that comes with them.

I try to think of the good stuff of them being here all the time. I get free entertainment, and become best friends with some of them, & they make me laugh. One of them in particular, I've been really close with is Ben, we just clicked in a way. He's so funny and it made me really sad when he left to go to school. He knows we're best friends, and since I have the same taste as a 5-year old boy, we get along great. Now his little sister, Willow, is coming to us and I can tell that we will be close too. I don't know if we will be as close as Ben and I are because that's a strong bond to beat, but we will see. Another kid is Clara. She says we're best friends, same with Eli. Then there's Kyle, Henry, and Lila. They either want to hang out with me 24/7 or totally ignore me, which is okay with me. There are a couple other kids who grew up and went to school or left, and there are a bunch of new kids who will be starting in the spring, so we will see how that goes.

My parents pretty much already know that I will not be providing kids for them ever. Mostly because of my mom's job. Not because of the kids, just the stuff they do. Unfortunately I've seen probably every fluid come out of a child ever. It's gross. I've seen how much they cry and can whine, and how annoying they can be. And you have to like to feed them, and take care of them and stuff all the time, which doesn't sound very time efficient to me. I do like kids but not if they are always there all the time. That's why I think I would be a good aunt to my brother's kids. Because I know he *loves* kids and will definitely have some. So I can hang out with them for like a few hours 2 days a week and then give them back. Which sounds pretty good to me.

CHAPTER SEVEN
Music

Today at school didn't actually suck. I was with my friends all day and just laughed, I haven't had that in so long. I think the 'don't care' mentality is a part of it. I didn't care that when I was laughing and smiling, people were judging me. Thinking that I was annoying and being obnoxious. But I didn't care. I didn't care because I was enjoying myself, I was attempting to be happy. And I don't think that I should be embarrassed for being happy? I remember last year if Ila, Morgan and I would be laughing and talking and these kids would always tell us to "shut up", "be quiet you're so loud" or "can you guys just text or something". We found their comments annoying but also funny, because they thought that we actually cared. Those kids were the kind of kids who thought they were really cool because they were mean. They had a clique and I don't think they were aware of how many people hated them. Since I've learned from that clique last year, I'm more okay with being judged for laughing. Something else that happened in school today is in English we got a new assignment and it's to write a persuasive essay. I've written essays before and I don't mind them, I'm pretty good at them. For this essay we get to choose our topic and you'll *never guess* what I chose. The education system. You're probably laughing right now because you know that I will go hard on this essay. This essay will prove my point right, that the education system is heavily flawed and needs to be changed. And anyone who wants to fight me on that, I live the life as do all my classmates, we have to deal with it. We have to suffer because of their errors and mistakesThis essay will be written well, very well. This is something I can debate about because I'm definitely passionate about it.

It's 7:09 pm and I just finished an hour of reading 'Every last word' by Tamara Ireland Stone. Only one book has ever made me cry, and it was because a dog died. But a lot of books have impacted me. One of them being Dear Evan Hansen, I bought that book randomly not knowing how much I'd relate to it. It's about a teen boy with anxiety and I think that after reading that I kind of understood what's going on with me. But anyway I was reading every last word, the main character has OCD and was having a panic attack. I cried a bit while reading it. Probably because I'm tired after school today but also just because I can relate to it so much. The way they described it felt so familiar to me, and I just felt so bad for them because I know that it sucks. It's like they were describing *exactly* what I go through when I freak out. It's almost comforting in a way. I haven't finished this book but I know it's going to be a favorite. I like to listen to music when I read. I don't know why, but it's almost comforting to have something in the background. AKA Taylor swift. Alastor can't stop the music, he can't prevent the comfort it gives me.

But I feel like I owe him something though. Or I deserve it, I deserve everything he does to me.

He gets to live and enjoy his life in my head when I deal with the unfairness of it. I look up to him in a way because he has power. He thinks I'm fine, it's something I can handle. I let him hold all the power, and I'm just some fragile person that he crushes down on.

But what if I leave alastor? I take out the knife he used to stab me in the back and I leave, I could do that. I can do that. He underestimates me, but yet he's still stronger than me. I just want to be the one with all the power. And like I said before he's a disease, an infection. Covering and drowning me. Taking over.

Not directed towards anyone just this is how it is. I'm trying. Even though it doesn't look like I'm trying, I am. I am trying so hard. I feel so hopeless, so much anger, I just want to be rid of him. Feel the relief in him finally being gone. Like washing him away, being clean, empty. Alastor being dead.

CHAPTER EIGHT
Pure embarrassment

I don't normally feel proud of myself for things but sometimes I do and it's normally for bigger things. When I reached my running goal, my essay that I wrote about the education system, I don't even know if it's good from my teacher's point of view but I was proud. Also I'm proud of this. Me writing to you, right now. It's hard to express how I'm feeling but when I'm writing it just comes right out, flows. I've always been a good writer ever since I was little but I was never so into it like I am now. I *want* to write whenever I can. A lot of people are passionate about things like their hobbies, like art or music, maybe sports too. Don't get me wrong I *love* running but not like I like writing. I'm totally in control of what I write, what kind of writing I want it to be, what it's about, I can express myself in my writing with over 171,476 words. Of course I don't use them all but I have the option to if I want. I love to write in any shape or form. I have a big imagination that can range from big to small and I'm proud of that. I can write anywhere. At any time. I'm really good at that and I'm not sure why but I like it. I could be sitting at the kitchen table and thinking of something so I pull out my phone, press the docs app, find Alastor and just start typing. That's what happens. But sometimes it's on the bus, in class, in my room while I'm doing something, or in the car. Which is where I am right now. Sometimes I plan when I want to write. Like I'm in hardcore writing mode so I plan 20-40 minutes in advance that I'm going to write. And I have to make sure the essentials are done. My room is clean, lights are off, everything I need for the next day is done, and my study music is playing on my Alexa. Once that's all done, I can sit and write for like an hour, maybe less, maybe more. In that time I write at least a page, sometimes even 3. But What encourages me to write? I would like to say that finishing this encourages me to write. Getting a new goal done. Done quick. But also I think it's not so much of an encouragement, more of a push. My problems push me to write, my anxiety pushes me to write. Alastor hates it because it's about him but whatever. This is a way to cope or to vent for me. So that's why I write. I wrote almost every day. I love writing too so that helps. When I started writing this I thought it was going to be like a *story* about my life, but it's turned into more of a journal and I like that. It doesn't have the same guidelines of a story. *So* when I started writing this it wasn't *about* Alastor. Of course he'd be mentioned but it was never going to be *mainly* about him like it is now. After writing a bit it kind of came clear that that's what this book should be about. This book wasn't always about him. And I also like that, because it's not always about him. It doesn't need to be.

Next day, I'm on the bus right now and all I'm thinking about is gym class. How embarrassing I was. I was actually happy for the most of it, until what happened, happened. We were playing floor hockey and I was having fun on a team with my friend Elle. But then I think I was getting so competitive and into it that I didn't realize I was being stupid. Looked stupid. I was running after the puck and it just kept rolling and rolling further and further away. Normal people would wait for it to stop so someone could pass it to them but I just kept trying to get it. And I ran after the puck for half a circle, I chased the puck in a C. After I just gave up because someone passed it to my team and I was standing there and just felt so unbelievable embarrassed and stupid. I just stood there and shrugged my shoulders so people thought I was upset, not embarrassed, maybe so they wouldn't feel bad or thought it was funny. But it wasn't funny to me. I analyze everything that happened in those moments and it sucks.

In these situations Alastor taunts me. He bullies me. Floating around me. Antagonizing me, all of that until I burst. I think I've always had anxiety. I obviously didn't know it then but now looking back it's so obvious. There was never a way we could've prevented alastor, he was always going to come. I think back to when one time I had to present in grade 5, I was probably around 10 or 11. I was up in front of the class and I was petrified. I knew what the feeling was that I had as I'd had it many times before but not that bad. I couldn't speak clearly and when I talked, I would stutter and my voice would tremble. I got that knot that I always get in my stomach. I was thinking that I was just nervous, no big deal. There was also another time when I was really into doing gymnastics. So my parents signed me up. I remember the first day was the worst. The car ride there the knot in my stomach got tighter and tighter. When I got there I knew someone from my school. I was literally dead. I felt embarrassed. I was on the lowest level and they were on the highest, so obviously I felt stupid. Anyways I did make a new friend and we hung out a few times and still kind of talked, that made it a bit better. But every single time I got ready and got into the car to go to gymnastics that horrible feeling came and never went away. I just remembered feeling so weird, thinking of the other kids were feeling that way. They probably weren't because they were normal 11 year olds. My parents didn't like it when I didn't go but I couldn't tell them that I was scared of going cause that makes no sense. My favorite memory of me joining anything was when I was three. My parents put me in ballet just like any three year old girl, and it didn't go so well. Obviously it isn't because alastor, he hasn't developed in my brain quite yet. But I walked in probably stayed there for 20 minutes until I ran out of the room calling all the other girls stupid. I don't know why but I think that's so perfect for me. Makes me laugh. But anyways, I've technically always had Alastair with me even 5 years ago. When I was *10*. It's hard to believe. I hadn't acknowledged him because I thought it was normal. All the other kids were like me. Eventually I realized it wasn't normal and I realized how bad it was getting.

Because it was getting pretty bad. If only a 13 year old me knew how bad it is now compared to it back then. Maybe I'll be saying that again when I'm a little older. Hopefully not but who knows.

CHAPTER NINE
Not feeling normal

I just got ready to go out with my friends for 'Galentines day'. I was super productive today but I got everything done so quick that I have hours before I could even start to get ready. Made me kind of anxious. But also bored out of mind. So I was doing everything I could to keep myself busy. It also didn't help that I'm excited to hang out with them. We haven't hung out with all 5 of us since October. Also we're getting food so that makes me excited too. We all are trying to wear red or pink, so I'm wearing blue mom jeans, a black tank top, and a red cardigan type sweater that's my moms. I'm also wearing my black hightop converse, a heart necklace, and 3 rings, one of them being my fidget ring. I normally don't get anxious with my friends but I do in public so I thought I'd wear it. I did my makeup all nice and straightened my hair too. So I don't feel as ugly anymore. All of us are giving each other valentines. I made some cute home made ones I found on Pinterest, and gave them all a little chocolate heart with it. It's simple but it's still cute. I'm actually writing this as I wait to be picked up. We're going to Boston pizza for dinner and then we're going to go back to Ila's house and watch a valentines movie and just hangout. I think I'll have fun.

That was two days ago, and I did have fun. I find that when I hangout with my friends I get out all this energy, this really crazy fun energy, then after a few hours I'm pooped and ready to go home and go to bed. I feel bad because my friends might think I'm neglecting them but I'm really just tired. But I always have fun, it just never lasts. Al never takes a day off or even a weekend. I'm not sure if seasonal depression is a thing but I feel like it could be. I don't know how winter affects mental health but who knows. Just lately everything is starting to feel like a task. I'm feeling lazy and tired. I don't want to do anything, anything at all. I just want to lay in bed and go to my phone. The tv is on, my lights are on, I have 5 better things I *should* be doing but I just lay here on my side curled up, and *not* caring. My eyes are heavy, the eye bags get darker, I start to eat too much or not enough. School is *so much* harder to go to when I'm like this. I feel like crying when I get like this, but then just tell myself, "You're just tired, that's why you're feeling emotional, you're just tired." I wish I could just *know* that I'm going to feel okay, I *want* to know that I'm not always going to be like this or think like this. I want to actually be okay. But I'm so flippin tired. I don't want to do anything, everything makes me tired, and I'm just so blank feeling. Numb almost. I find that I'm numb feeling a lot. Just staring into nothing, day dreaming but my mind is blank. I think it's because I'm tired maybe, or just simply done. Bored of Alastor in a way. I'm so used to him that it's become numb. When I get anxious I realize how not numb I am. Because every time it feels new in a way. But also not because I'm so hectic in my head. You know when you're at a party and everyone is talking? Well maybe not a party, I've never been to a party before, but in tv shows and movies. At parties you just hear a bunch of people's voices overlapping each other's. That's what it sounds like in my head. But it's louder and all my voice. But it doesn't sound like me totally. Almost slightly different. But I think it's because it's Alastor. My voice doesn't sound the same because it's not truly mine. It's his. The want to just lay down and do nothing or sleep is strong when I get like this. But lately my want to do nothing or sleep is something I want to do *all* the time. Not just when I get like this. I'm not quite sure what's going on, but I'm not normal these days. Not feeling normal in the least.

SMALL UPDATE

It's almost two months into 2022 and I would say I'm doing pretty good with my goals. I wanted to write more in this and I have, I'm pretty much two chapters ahead of where I wanted to be. I also have been washing my face every night and every morning, which was one of my biggest goals. I used to be bad at that, not taking care of myself. Another one of my goals was to make my bed every morning, and I would say I'm doing it about half the time. Because some mornings I'm just so tired, I sleep in then I don't have enough time to make my bed. Also the working out goal hasn't really been a successful one. I've been busy and the free time I do have I just want to do nothing and chill. But I have been eating better. Instead of grabbing the quickest snack I make a better healthier one. And lastly, to fill free time with hobbies instead of phones, is actually working really well. Better than I thought it would. Which is good.

CHAPTER TEN
Medicated

In the third grade I wrote a mini book called "feels". I was like eight or nine. The book was about feelings hence the title. It basically talked about the emotions I was going through back then. Sad, happy, angry, left out, ugly. And along with those feelings I said ways you could fix the bad feelings, make it better. I remember being so proud of myself writing it, making a fancy new copy. I think it's cute, looking back. It's also funny because the grammar and spelling mistakes make it all so much better. But I also look at how things really haven't changed. Or how they looped right back. Because about 5 years later, here I am writing a book about feelings. Except the difference is that I'm older, this is a *real* book, and there's no grammar mistakes, for the most part. Another difference is that this book isn't so much about feelings either it's about Al, but he has a lot to do with my feelings so I think it's close enough. I just think it's so perfect. Naturally I would fall back into what I started with. Writing. The only difference is back then it was "feels" now it's Alastor. It's hard to get rid of habits like this, but this habit is a good one, and I'm glad I'm getting so into it again. I've never been like this. Looking forward to 10 minutes of free time to write. Writing down ideas so excitedly because they just randomly popped in my head and I don't want to forget them. I like that. And something else that I always think about is how wrong it is in 'writing' to be saying 'you' like I'm talking to whoever is reading, the 'reader'. And I think that the way I've written this whole thing is wrong and not good. But then I remember that it's supposed to be that way. I AM writing to YOU. That's kind of like the whole point. Well not the *whole* point, but a big part of it. I'm writing to you about Alastor, explaining stuff that's going on. I don't really know who is reading this because I find it hard to think that people would *want* to read this, but whatever. Every time I write, it's not to Alastor, to myself, or to google docs, it's to *you*. I think about you while writing. Hoping you can relate, feel less alone. So I'm choosing to say no, that the way I'm writing isn't wrong, it's right. Everything is circumstantial, and this is. Because I'm literally writing to you. I'd like to think that this is good enough that at least a handful of people would want to read it, and they liked it. I understand that most people wouldn't like it. Everyone has an opinion and I completely respect their opinion, I can see how they wouldn't like my writing, it makes sense. But I just hope and wish that there are at least like 5 people who aren't my friends or family that truly like it. They don't have to love it & think it's amazing but just at least like it & think it's good. That would make me happy, and so proud. Since we're thinking back. When I think back to like a year ago I never would have thought that I'd be taking medication. I never thought that my brain was messed up, or "Unbalanced" enough for me to be medicated. But now taking my meds every night is routine, it's normal. It's just bizarre to me that not too long ago, going on meds seemed weird. The way I saw it was you have to be really not good in the head or crazy to be on that kind of medication. But now, it's normal to be on medication, tons of people are on it. Especially at my age. I don't know any kids on medication but I know there are some. It's sad that kids this young are on pills, but what can you do? Sometimes taking my meds is a pain. It feels useless. Like a chore. I could be all nice and comfy in bed ready to go to sleep then I remember

I forgot to take my meds. And I have to get up, take out my orange 100 sertraline & take it with water. Next my 25 yellow sertraline & take that with water. And lastly my tiny 1g Aripiprazole, it's almost like a light green color. I take one drink of water to finish it off then go back to being comfy. Some nights aren't like that, I take them a bit early and don't have to worry about forgetting and having to get up. Which is nice. A lot of the time I don't even know why I'm taking meds, I don't really know if they're even working.

CHAPTER ELEVEN
'Back when'

I was looking back at old pictures and I guess I don't realize how different I am. I'm a totally different person. I don't know who the girl in the pictures is but she looks happy. I want to go back there. But I know I can't, like saying 'there is no way to move but forward'. It's true. I just hope that I can get to a good place in my head where I am now. Looking back at old pictures is so weird because I see all these friends I used to have. Every time I scroll there's a new face and a new smile. I don't talk to almost everyone I was friends with back then. Even a year ago, I wasn't friends with those people. Right now I have Ila and Morgan obviously. And Ella and Charlotte. I don't talk to Charlotte much cause she's not in my class, but we still hangout. Ila, Morgan and Ella are *all* in my class so I talk to them almost everyday if not everyday. I have good friends right now and I'm really lucky to have such good friends. But anyways looking through the photos you can see such a massive difference from me before lockdown and after lockdown. Lockdown was the highlight of my covid experience. Even though I never had covid. I absolutely LOVED lockdown. I was living the life. Me and my family were really close then we would hang out together and eat together every night. I wore whatever I wanted, whatever was comfiest. And you're not going to believe this, but I stayed up till like midnight every night and slept until 11. Doesn't sound like me right? I was not doing too good in school, I normally finished my work *just* in time or not at all. We also started to redo my room during quarantine. My brother moved into the 'shed' which isn't a shed, just a big bedroom outside the house. And I got his room so we broke down the wall in between our rooms and I got one big room. Renovating my room and his room made us less bored. Gave us something to do. It was fun. We actually did a lot of renovating in the whole house during quarantine. Quarantine is also where I started to get into makeup and special effects makeup. Looking at my old makeup I'm embarrassed. It was so bad but I thought it was amazing back then. It's kind of funny. You can see my progress big time. My coffee addiction got worse, I started to get taller and slimmer, also I got VERY antisocial. My social anxiety got worse, so going back to school after that was horrible. My mum says that as much as I loved quarantine it fed the beast, (aka Alastor). Made my anxiety worse. In quarantine I couldn't get the help I wanted in the way that I wanted, over the phone was an option but I didn't like that. So I kind of just went through quarantine mildly struggling. It wasn't bad, just something hiding in the back of my mind waiting. Eventually Alastor introduced himself and it got way worse. There wasn't much for me to do. I tried to journal but that didn't work. I hated it. My family and I technically are Christian. But we never practiced it. In quarantine I often found myself praying, praying but not knowing who I'm praying to. Praying I'll feel better, praying I'll be fine, just a rough patch. I thought and thought about god and heaven a lot more after that. And I realized I'm not Christian and I don't believe in that. Not because when I prayed nothing happened. But because it's just not what I believe in, it doesn't seem practical to me. When we die I think we just die. And I don't think that a man created earth and trees and animals. I think it's science. There isn't enough proof for me to believe that God or Jesus exist. At least not right now. I think they definitely *were* people who *did* live but a long time ago. They also were probably great guys who did amazing things, I just don't think they did everything Christian's say they did. But that is just *my* belief and *my* opinion. My mom isn't religious. I don't really think she has one, my dad does believe that there is a god or gods, I have no clue what my brother is, and my friends are mostly Atheists like me, or are religious just don't practice it. My Nan does believe in God. I don't know how much she does but she does go to church sometimes on Christmas Eve but she's not a hard core Christian. I'm not sure what my Aunt is, and my dad's parents are religious but not sure what about. I totally respect anyone and everyone's religion. You know you do you, I don't really care. It doesn't make me not like you just because of your beliefs. Everyone is entitled to their own beliefs and opinions. But, one thing I do not like when it comes to religion is when people question you or try to tell you your belief is wrong. I don't mind if someone respectfully asks why even though it's not their business, at least they're nice about it. But no one has the right to say you're wrong for what you believe in. Death is a big thing with religion. Every religion believes something different will happen to you when you die, I just think you die. Plain and simple. Death was a big thing with me. Two years ago, so 12 turned 13. I was so afraid of death and dying. The 'not knowing' of it all. I used to think about it all the time. I had a hard time sleeping because of it. I'd stay up late crying out of fear. I was scared of running out of time. Like I'm wasting my time. I'm still scared of wasting time. Not as much but I am. Wasting it on being sad and anxious. But I don't really care about death and dying anymore. It happens every day, it's inevitable. But I want to die of old age and hopefully in my sleep. I also want to do so many crazy things before I die but I will mostly do those as a young adult. Travel, zip lining, jump off a bridge. Plus so much more. And if I knew it was my last day, I'd want to spend it doing my favorite things, like writing, cooking, eating, makeup, running. And more important spending time with my animals, friends, and family. Just keep it simple. This isn't totally related but someone I want to meet, dead or alive, is Stan Lee. Marvel comics creator. He sadly passed away but if I could meet him I would just ask him hundreds of questions I have about Marvel and all the superheroes. I would also LOVE to meet all the actors who play them. Like the original 6 avengers to spider man, Scarlet witch black, panther. I'd love to meet them all. One time I actually had a dream that I met Robert Downey jr, Scarlett Johansson, & Chris Evans. I woke up being really disappointed that I hadn't. But I can see me & Stan Lee having an in depth conversation about the comics at a cafe with coffee.

CHAPTER TWELVE
Mopey

I would like to say I'm a pretty observant person, especially when I observe people. Like the kids in my class. I won't use their real names. But there's this big friend group, all guys then one girl. I used to be friends with this girl. I was really close with her when we were little but she's changed a lot. A lot of the people I know from when I was little changed a lot but I haven't. They've mostly changed for the worse but I don't know if it's good that I haven't changed. It's probably not. Anyways, this friend group is really loud and most of the time they're funny but sometimes they get on my nerves. They can be obnoxious. Some of them come to school high from whatever they smoked. They think it's really cool. Some don't, and if they do you can't tell. There's one guy in the friend group who's really quiet, on his phone all the time instead of hanging out with his friends. All you see is the big group of friends and he's at his desk on his phone.

Makes me wonder a bit. Why, why he's so quiet, maybe he's just on his phone a lot or maybe he's like me. Anxious. This friend group can either be nice to you or pick fun at you. They can make a joke that really hurts even if it wasn't meant to. I haven't had to deal with that but someone close to me did. I felt horrible. Besides this friend group there are these two kids. I've known them forever and they're pretty nice to me, but one of them isn't so nice to Ila. For whatever reason, they just don't like Ila. It's so weird though because they don't even try to hide it. Pretend they like her. There is another group, smaller. Just girls and they aren't too popular or anything but they seem pretty nice, smart. One of them gets kind of bullied in a way by the big friend group. But she doesn't really know it. They crack these jokes at her or about her and I think she feels included almost in their click but it's the opposite. They're making fun of her. It's kind of sad. There are a ton of other kids in my class, but they're all quiet. I don't want to say they aren't interesting because I don't know them. I observe Ila, Morgan and Ella too. See who they're looking at, what they are paying attention to, what they hear that they don't like, or what they hear that they do like or find funny. It helps me know what to say and what not to say. I don't want to offend them in anyway, or make them think I'm stupid. I care what everyone thinks of me, but I'll only do something about it because of my friends and family. If that makes any sense.

It's 6:29 and it's a school night tonight. Something I hate. School nights stress me out. I have to make sure I have no homework to do and if I do I have to do it. I need to make lunch and coffee for the next day. I have to have my outfit laid out with my fidget ring ready to go. I also *need* to have all my outfits planned for the whole week or I'm unprepared. I need to have all my 'chores' done. So laundry, clean room, and my backpack, AirPods, mask, binder, & shoes ready for the next day. I have to have *at least* 1 hour before bed to mentally prepare myself for who knows what, my face and teeth need to be clean, my meds need to be taken and I need to have my noise machine on and my lights off. An exception for my nightlight. This all has to be done by 8:30, *maybe* 9:00. I know this all sounds stupid but it's true. It has to be like this or you can't go to school the next day. Nothing can go out of plan, because then it's not right. It's messy & just wrong. But now it's 6:38 and I haven't done any of those things let alone eat dinner. I'm sick to my stomach about going to school tomorrow, and I don't know why. Normally I'm not like this, I'm never like this. I don't know what's so different about tomorrow. I feel like I'm going to vomit, my head hurts, my eyes hurt and I'm beyond exhausted. I don't know what's going on. But it's 20 to 7 and I still need to do my homework, plan my outfits, get my bag ready with all my other stuff, pack lunch and coffee, clean my room, & get ready for bed. But I don't feel like doing any of it. I don't *want* to do any of it. I feel depressed almost lately. Not myself. Right now I feel like crying, throwing up and screaming. Maybe not all at the same time, but you get the idea. I just feel so frustrated. So angry. My head is something I can't fix. Alastor is something I can't fix. Can't get rid of it. Ugh I'm getting myself worked up. I'm just so tired of it. Like I said before everything is becoming a chore, a task I don't want to do. I've become lazy and I'm in a slump. A gross one. But even though I've become like this I still get so anxious, probably more anxious than normal. Because since I'm not doing these things or putting them off, Alastor likes to bug me about that. Putting all the bad scenarios in my head. Then I rush to do these things last minute and become worn out & drowsy.

I went to my mom's room and just laid on her bed. She knew I wasn't feeling good. She asked me a couple of questions, I can't remember any of them because my mind was blurry. I could feel my eyes filling up with tears and drop from my eye down my cheek to her pillow. She couldn't see my face but I think she knew I was crying. I told her I was just frustrated and tired. I didn't go into detail. The only way that she can't keep up with what's going on is by reading this. It's the only way I can talk about what's going on. There have been many times that I've cried while writing. I just wrote what I'm feeling and then I started crying without even knowing. I hate crying. Makes me feel so weak. My mom said she will try to get me to see Samantha or Lisa soon. They are the people that I talk to. Samantha I just talk to her about what's going on and she talks back to me. But Lisa teaches me how to cope and deal. How to get over it, learn to live with it. I went back to my room to take off my smudged mascara then I went to wash my face. I just laid in my bed after that. Watched tv. My mum caught up on her reading of this. And came to talk to me saying that I know I think I'm crazy but I'm not. A lot of people feel the way I do. I know both of these things, but they don't really seem to do much. I think people tell me that too often. It wears out when you hear it so much. But anyways, that was last night. I'm home from school today. I'm absolutely exhausted. I'm in a slump. I want it to be summer. And I realized something I do when I'm not feeling too well in the head. My hearing is on but the words aren't resonating in my head. My eyesight is almost the same thing, I can see but not paying attention or realizing what I see. Never noticed that till last night.

Also I don't want this to be a sad book when people read it. I don't want people to feel mopey after reading it. Thinking "wow life sucks" or "this is life?". I don't want that. I want it to be more of a learning book. Learning what it's like to have anxiety. What it's like to have an alastor. I want people to be like "omg I know that feeling" or "wow I didn't know other people felt like that too". I want it to be relatable. Tough times come and go, and I'm a teenager with imbalanced chemicals in my brain, so I'm having tough times right now. But I'm hoping I won't be like this forever and if I am, it won't be this bad. It shouldn't be. You have to learn to deal with it, live with it. Not let it get to you. I just haven't learned any of that yet. But I am trying, I really am. I'm just so frickin' tired. I'm on the bus right now and my eyes are so heavy. I could fall asleep right now. Later in class I feel the same. But my friends are talking to me so every time I try to put my head down I have to bring it back up again so they don't think I don't care. I do care though, I'm just tired. But I don't want to be rude so I pay attention.

CHAPTER THIRTEEN
Unbelievably exhausted

I'm planning on publishing this. Obviously, I'm not done yet because you're still reading. My plan is to publish it as an Ebook on Apple Books and Kobo. I need to price it and make a cover & stuff which I can do myself. But there's a bunch of legal stuff I need help with, the copyright stuff too. Apple & Kobo take 30% of what you make. Which is really good because you get 70% still and don't have to pay anything. I also need to make a website, or fix the one I have. I'm so happy and kind of shocked that I'm publishing this. It just seems so crazy. I never would have thought I'd publish a book let alone write one. It seemed so hard. Even though I'm so happy, I'm also completely terrified. I'm kind of putting my whole life out there for everyone to read. Most of the people who I think will read it already know a lot of this but it's the people that don't know this stuff, and then *will* know about it that scares me. But I'll be fine, as long as this book does help some people. I'm over half way done so I have plenty of time to figure everything out. After this chapter I only have three more planned chapters. But I might write more than expected so it might span out into 10 chapters instead of 8. And by the looks of everything I might actually have to add on those two chapters. I didn't realize how quick I was writing. I wasn't supposed to write chapter 5 until towards the end of March and beginning of April. But it's the end of February right now. So I'm a month ahead of where I'm supposed to be. I also have certain chapters dedicated to certain topics I want to talk about, but I just think of random things I want to write about and write about them. You would've thought I'd run out of things to write about. But nope.

I like to look at my favorite books, compare them to Alastor. But I can't do that at all because I'm only 15, have no clue what I'm doing, & totally inexperienced. And the people who are writing these books are professional and not writing it in the same context as me. I look at Dear Evan Hansen, a favorite of mine. And I absolutely love that book. Everything about it is so good. But then they made it into a movie, a musical. That is the last book that I can see being turned into a musical. I think that kind of ruined it for me. Even though I haven't actually *seen* the movie, and I'm kind of not planning on seeing it either. I don't want that book to be *completely* ruined for me. I'm sure it's a good movie for people who haven't read the book because there's no context there, but for those who have read it, probably wouldn't like it. But the book I'm reading now, Every Last Word, is SO good. I can see it being my new favorite. Probably because I relate to the book so much, but it's also just such a good book. When I'm on a roll reading, I'm on a roll. I just zip right through it. I actually have a lot of books that I'm excited to read. I have a few just sitting on my shelf. The Midnight Library, All the Bright places, A Good Girls Guide to Murder, & The Secret History. All of those waiting to be read. I'm sure all of them will be good. I'm hoping that someone could think of Alastor that way. Or maybe a future book of mine. I hope to write more. Like I said I'm only 15 and it can only get better from here right?

People probably find it hard to believe I have anxiety. Especially the kids in my class. They would think that I'm lying or faking it or something. I don't see why anyone would want to take something like that, maybe for attention. But attention is the last thing I want. The reason that they probably think I couldn't have anxiety is because I can be loud. Like in class when I'm with Ila Morgan and Ella. I get loud and I laugh when I'm with them. Or if I'm excited or if I'm mad about something I get loud. Not intentionally, I just do. Also I bring coffee to school a lot and it gets me really hyper, and it distracts me, makes me unfocused. But if I don't bring coffee I'm miserably tired. Everything I do or say at school haunts me later. Later like maybe 5 minutes later, 1 hour, on the bus home, AT home, before I go to sleep. That one happens to me a lot. It seems that every mistake I've ever made likes to torment me before I go to bed. Makes me cringe. My friends see me SO differently than everyone else. They see me as this funky crazy weird girl who says "live a little" to pretty much everything. They see me as someone who is pretty clueless, but smart in school. They think I'm addicted to drugs and coffee. But they obviously know it's just a joke. The kids in my class probably think I do drugs, like for real. Just in the way we talk about it. But my friends also see me as calm, tired, and chill, they know I don't present & hate but love confrontation. They also know they can talk to me about anything and I'll try to help them. They know I'm shy and need someone to ask the teachers questions I don't feel comfortable asking. But, the kids in my class don't know those two versions of me. They probably think I'm some annoying & stupid kid in their class. I feel like they all hate me. And I say all but it's not all of them it's that one big group of friends that some would consider the "popular kids". I have no clue why I care so much about what they think of me. Because I'm sure they don't care that I find them annoying and obnoxious. But I care about what everyone thinks of me, not just them. I think that's just a part of what comes with Alastor. But at the same time I'm so carefree. I don't care if they think I'm weird or annoying or loud. That sounds like a them problem. The times that they think I'm annoying is probably when I'm happiest at school. Because I'm laughing with my friends, I'm having fun. So it sucks for them if they are annoyed but atleast I was happy & having fun.

You know those days were probably the best days I had at school. But I like to think of what would actually be a good day at school, the ideal day. I think that I would have gym, art, civics (so we can see Mrs C), and we have math and English every day. But math would be better if I was just fooling around with Ila and Ella. Morgan actually does her work so she wouldn't be fooling around. English would be good if I could write anything or read my book. And I would have a good lunch, my coffee would taste good. I would feel comfortable in my outfit, mentally and physically. I wouldn't be tired, or feel like everyone is judging me. I wouldn't have homework or tests to worry about. That would be the perfect day at school. The worst day of school isn't hard to accomplish. I'd be tired, have math, science, health, English, & family studies. My lunch & coffee would suck. My friends just do their work quietly while I sit at my desk with my head down. I'd feel like everyone is judging me or talking badly about me. Which no one does, I'm not cool enough or relevant enough to be talked about. I would have homework and a test the next day. And lastly to top it off I'd probably have a panic attack. I've had many days that were like that. They are not fun. That's why I hate going to school. You never know what kind of day you're going to have. It's the fear of not knowing what kind of day it'll be. The fear of not knowing is a big one for me.

Alastor

Right now I'm on the brink of tears & the only thing I think to do is write. Why? I don't know. It's become so natural for me. To just write when I have a problem. Write it away. I feel like the words are worn out. I. Am. Tired. I'm exhausted, overtired, weary, sleepy, worn out, fatigued, drained, & drowsy. And most of all, irritated. I'm irritated that I'm tired that no amount of coffee will fix it. I'm irritated that I'm always going to be this tired. I write this as the frustration builds and the tears fall. I know that other people have it worse I know. But I can't help it. I know that I have to learn to live with it, because that's what everyone tells me. But I'm tired of having to learn to live with it. I'm tired. I just feel like giving up. Refusing to leave bed in the morning, becoming careless of my work and my chores. Stop socializing. Stop eating. I *could* do that. Right now I *want* to do that. But I can't, because alastor wont let me. And he makes me so mad because of that. I'm so mad right now. So angry. So angry he's not a physical being that I can punch in the face. So angry that the only way I can be mean to him is by being mean to myself. Ugh Words can't describe the level of frustration I have right now. I'm just stuck. My hands are tied. I have to keep living in this exhausting cycle. It's tiring. And I *hate* it when people get mad at me for thinking I'm just skipping school just to skip. Like oh my god. I'M TIRED. I'm tired of it. If you can get rid of Alastor I'm sure this wouldn't be a problem. But that'll be pretty hard cause he sure likes me a lot. God. How come boys at my school don't like me the way Alastor does? Life would be a lot easier if they and Alastor switched places. I can't find enough ways to describe the exhaustion I'm feeling. I'm curled up on my bed in the dark writing to no one. Ha, how pathetic am I? This would be a good time to go on a run. Crying with the wind hitting my face. Running is the safest but yet most risky thing I can do. The adrenaline you feel while running is amazing. It feels good. But, nothing bad can happen to me. You know besides getting murdered or kidnapped. But I've convinced myself that I could handle myself out there. But there's no way for me to get a panic attack while running. I'm okay. But because of the stupid snow, ice, and freezing temperature I can't run and probably won't be able to until April. Which makes things worse. I have nothing right now that will guarantee that this feeling will be gone. And I know for a fact that it won't, because I feel like this every day. Today I'm just tired enough, emotional enough, and just so sick of it that it affects me way more. But I guess to sum that all up, I'm pretty tired. If you couldn't tell. Twinkie could tell I was off. I laid down next to her and she immediately started head butting me and purring. I got up to look at her and she got up too, her head butted my face and kind of grossly licked my chin. It's the thought that counts. She is misunderstood. She's way sweeter than people think she is.

I stayed home today, because of exhaustion. My mom isn't too pleased about it. She knows I've done good with catching up on work. I always have done good. I have 90s in all my classes except for 2, which is math and science. And I've never been good at math or science. But I have a 70 in math and an 81 in science. I'm not failing. But whenever I stay home I don't do my makeup & I wear ratty clothes. So I often think that the parents of the kids my mom takes care of. I think they think I look like crap. They have to be thinking "what the heck did she go through" or "looks like she got hit by a bus". You know for me to look like that one day is no big deal, everyone has a bad day. But I stay home at least once a week and every day I stay home I look the same. Big eye bags on my run down face, hair a mess, and the saddest looking clothes. And when

I look like this I look skinny. I ALWAYS think I look chubby. Always. I grew up with kids at my school calling me fat and it kind of just stuck. They don't anymore they haven't since we got to middle school. But I still feel that way. No matter how much I lose or gain Weight I'll always feel that way. I've lost so much weight over the past year. Like 14 pounds worth. I'm 98 pounds. I know that's not healthy but I'm okay with it. I *was* 112 pounds but Alastor made me lose it all. I tell people that I'm just thinning out, like my brother. My brother got really tall and skinny. So I just say that so am I. But I know that's not true. I've grown like what two or three inches? He grew like 7. I probably eat the same amount as the kids my mom takes care of. Just add a ton of coffee into that diet.

CHAPTER FOURTEEN
Safe space

Morgan's birthday is coming up really soon. I got her some small twisted textured hoops and a bubble ring. I also got her an anti stress bath bomb, two bags of candy and some pens that she likes. I made her a homemade card and I put all of this in an Avengers lunch box I got for her. I thought she'd find that funny. I love giving gifts, it's fun. To make people smile. Ila's birthday is coming up soon too towards the end of March. I'm getting her a diffuser and a three pack of essential oils. The oils are for sleep, relaxing, & stress relief. I thought she'd like those. I'll probably give her some candy too. Birthdays are always fun but mostly when it's other people's birthdays.

It's now March 4th, Morgan's birthday! I wished her a happy birthday on message and Instagram. But I didn't go to school today because last night was an event. Everything was fine, I finished my book, it was amazing, got ready for school the next day, and got ready for bed. But I was in bed overthinking for like an hour then all of a sudden I got really bad heartburn, and I felt like I might throw up. But, I wasn't nauseous or anything, I just felt like something might come up from the back of my throat. I texted my mum and she said to take some tums. I took a total of three in the 3 hours I was struggling with heat in my chest. But my parents said it might be acid reflux because that's what it sounded like. So I googled things to help with it and it said baking soda water. So I had some of that and it was nasty, I waited like 30 minutes for that to do nothing. I researched some more and it said apple cider vinegar. So, I took out the apple cider vinegar and took a shot of that. I didn't know that it would activate the baking soda I just had because I didn't know it could do that. But it can, I threw up like a minute later. Most of it was clear, which is good. After that I didn't feel as bad so I went to bed, google said to lay off my left so I did. But I was up until 1:00 in the morning thinking I was going to puke again and I *hate* puking. It's a fear of mine. But eventually I fell asleep. This morning when I talked to my mum and told her what I did to help, she laughed at me because of course I threw up o duh. But I have no regrets. It made me feel better. But anyways I'm feeling way better today. I just feel like I need to burp a lot which is weird. But I'm getting anxious for Morgan's birthday. I know I'll have fun and I have nothing to worry about because it's the same friends I hang out with all the time. Charlotte, Ila, & Morgan obviously, and me. Minus Ella because we just found out she got covid. Out of the 5 of us, Me and Charlotte are the only ones left standing. Tonight we're going for sushi then back to Morgan's house for cupcakes and presents. I LOVE getting people presents, unless Im not really close with them. I like buying people presents rather than getting them. I just love getting them something that will make them smile or laugh or getting them something they've been really wanting. It's just so fun.

It's the morning after, I had a really good time and I think Morgan did too. But I think we were all tired. You could tell. We all were so go go go for sushi and presents but once it got to hangout time we were tired. Makes me tired thinking of how I was tired. Anyways the sushi was really good, so were the cupcakes, and I think we all had fun. Morgan liked her presents which is good. I was more excited to give her the present than she was to open it. But it was good. Now I feel like I got hit by a bus. Hanging out is a lot of work. It's tiring. But today is a chore day so I have to get them done. Sweep & mop my floors, clean my table tops, wash my bedding and put new clean sheets on, & do my laundry. I do this every weekend. It's routine, or ritual-like. I have to do it. If people ask me to make plans on my chore day I can't go, because it has to get done. It's important to me to feel clean. Also the cat barfed on my bed so I kind of had to wash them today.

People think it's kind of weird how I'm so good at keeping my room tidy. But it'd be a shame not to because it's my favorite place ever & it would be disrespectful almost. My room is a rectangular shape and has two decent sized windows on the back wall. When you walk in my bed is to the left and it's pretty big, tall and fluffy looking. On my bed I have a bunch of pillows, Cornelius jr (my big bear), and a weighted blanket at the bottom of my bed. Above my bed I have fake vines hanging randomly, but I like it. Next to my bed I use this ikea cart as a nightstand. It has a tiny salt rock lamp and my charger on it. Beside that there is a indent in the wall almost, it's supposed to be a closeted so I put my dresser in

Alastor

there. On the wall where my door is I have a mirror on an area rug with some pretty prints on the wall. On the right side of my room I have a big toe in the middle of the wall with a cubical underneath with more clothes in there. I have another salt rock lamp, a diffuser, plants, and random stuff on there too. On one side of this wall I have my plant corner where I have three of my plants, one hanging. I have a fake vine hanging from there too, along with a picture and one of the two records I have on both sides of my tv. Underneath one of my windows is my desk, I have my jewelry, a candle, & a vase on there along with my mirror. I don't use my desk as a desk. I use it for makeup. I sit there to do it. Now we've made a circle back to the end of my bed. On the floor at the end of my bed is a basket for my extra throw blankets, and next to it is a shoe basket. In the very middle of my room is a beam that goes right in from the wall to the ceiling back to the wall. I have these really cool lights hanging on them. They're pretty. That's it. That's the room I love so much. And you may be confused as to why, but you'd just have to be there. It's a pretty big room & it's spacious. It's always clean. It's minimalist but cozy. I prefer the way my room looks at night. With my lights. I also love the fact that you'll find the weirdest things in my room. I have a grandma turtle made out of a seashell. Tiny tiny coke bottles. Little button people all around my room in random spots. I have a tea drawer, snack drawer, and a BB gun. Just random things. But I love that. Makes it fun. My room is comforting. My favorite place. I know I'll be sad when I leave for university but I'll make wherever I am next just as cozy, clean, weird, yet cute. I can do whatever I want in my room. Because it's mine. And I just can't use words to describe how much I love my room. I love it when people compliment me on it when they come over. Makes me proud. My room is actually probably the only thing I'm truly proud of. And this book will most likely be next. I find I'm super overprotective of my room & my things. I HATE it when things get ruined, ripped, stained or broken. I'm terrified of it. I don't know why because it's all replaceable. I can get a new one. Unless I can't but normally I don't let those irreplaceable things come close to harm. It freaks me out though. That I have attachment issues to non special objects. These things mean so much to me. But why? They're just things. I hold onto everything.

CHAPTER FIFTEEN
"Expressing stuff sucks"

I think the hardest thing for me to do every day is just getting up. Especially for school. I don't see a point because there seems like no reason to get out of bed. I don't see a point in getting up and living a depressing day that would be better at home in my room. I don't see a point in going to school that I'm being criticized and judged, a school that makes me jittery or isn't even educating me. I don't really see the point to living either. Not that I don't want to be alive, because I'm grateful. But what's the point of life? I don't see one. Why am I alive right now? Why do people live to suffer? What is the point? I hate the feeling in the morning when my alarm goes off. Not because I want to sleep more, because I'm dreading the day to come. The days that bring me near tears, the days that put so much pressure on me that I'm tense. I dread the feeling of going through another day of exhaustion and worry, a day of feeling criticized for the way I look, sound, and do things. A dreadful day of Alastor whispering in my ear non stop. A day that feels just like yesterday and the day before that, and how it will feel tomorrow. I hate the thought of having to get up and leave the place I'm most comfortable and safe to go to the most threatening place I've ever been. A place where I feel unprotected & in danger. What should I do? I'm exhausted from trying. I *want* to be better, but I don't know how to get there. I'm just so done, done with trying, done with Alastor, done with pushing & faking it away. I'm done. I'm so used to Alastor that it feels normal. This is *my* normal. And I hate that. I give up. I also think more adults need to open their eyes and realize that their child isn't okay. Some parents don't understand mental health and that drives me nuts. Obviously my parents do, but most don't. Most parents don't understand that some kids just need a mental health day. Not for any specific reason, they just do, parents do too. It's normal to just take a day, a break to regroup. It doesn't mean that something big and bad is wrong, just a little break. Parents need to pay attention to their child. And how they are doing, who they hang out with, how much they are eating, how long they are on their phone. It's not hard to just check in. Mental health is just as important as your physical health. Parents need to educate themselves. Kids aren't the same as they were 'back in the day' they've evolved, they've changed. Especially with phones and social media, *everything* is different because now, your child's life is on the internet for everyone out there to hold a microscope over them and pick at all their insecurities. Social media is also a great place for cyber bullying, your kid will get bullied virtually and I know it sucks because I've been there. People DMing me telling me im ugly or fat, no one likes me. Im annoying and stupid, ive heard it all. You need to actually take care of your kid, physically and mentally. You should be there for them, let them know that. Make sure they're comfortable talking with you when they need to, they're comfortable everywhere in your home, they don't hide away in their bedroom. A lot of parents just don't get it and I'm thankful that I don't have to deal with that because I can tell it sucks and I'm sorry for those who have to deal with it. Expressing stuff sucks too. like I know crying is something that makes you human but I hate it when I cry. Especially in front of others. Just today stuff happened and I was with my brother. I was trying *so* hard to hold back my tears because I so badly wanted to be seen as strong. But all I feel is weak, weak and sensitive. Every time I feel like crying in front of someone I try not to, so I seem tougher than I am. But when no one is around it's such a relief to just be able to cry. Cry and not feel weak and pathetic. I am allowed to just cry when I'm alone. Crying makes my cheeks flushed and hot, my lips puffy, my eyes welled up big & red. Every time I breathe in it's not steady, it's shaking with an unnerving feeling. My heart drops and is like a pit in my stomach, I feel like yelling and screaming but nothing comes out. People say time flies when you're having fun, it also flies by when you're crying. I think because everything is so hectic and crazy. Which is what it's like most of the times I've cried. Other times it's slow, very slow. I think it's because you're so miserable that everything seems to last longer. After I'm done crying which takes a really long time because once I start crying I can never stop. My face is so dry and feels so stiff, I'm congested and pooped. I'm completely exhausted after because it's so tiring, I don't know why because tears just fall from my eyes and I breathe a lot. But how can that make me so tired? I know it's mentally exhausting but still. Something my brother said to me during this was along the lines of life sucks, and this is life, you have to live through it. It was something like that, my mind was in such a blur that I can't remember. But when he said that I got sad. Because life has ups and downs and I definitely experienced the downs, big and small. But it's supposed to have ups and I have yet to experience many. I have had little ones but not very many big ones. I'm not angry that he said this, I'm more angry because it's true. He was being honest. I don't like that this one little comment he tried to use to make me feel better made me feel worse. I don't like that I over analyze and overthink things. It's annoying. Can I not just listen and let it sink in? Why do I have to think about every single low part in my 15 year old life that I've experienced, and struggle to find the highs? And I know this is random but I feel like I know myself pretty well. I know everything about myself. How I'll react to certain things. How I won't react to certain things. Things that I like, hate, love. But something that still doesn't make sense to me is that when someone who doesn't know me, doesn't know my story, my mindset. Assume something about me. Think they know me so well, well enough to say what they think the 'truth' is about me. They are just being honest, right? But no. The things people say hurt so much. Why do they hurt so much? Why do they break me? Shatter me to pieces. Because they don't know me. They don't know me at all. Maybe that's why it hurts so much. They don't know me. And because they don't know me, they say things that aren't true about me. It is painful to hear. But I think it's true. It hurts to not feel known by those you care about. Or maybe those you don't even care for. It feels nice to just feel understood. Until you realize that no one understands you. Clearly not feeling the best today.

I feel ugly today too. Like more ugly than normal. I have two pimples on my forehead and maybe a third will come. Normally I have clear skin but every now and again I get some. I hate it. It's mostly because of stress, diet, or hormones. It's a marking day at school today so we have the day off. I'm in the living room with the littles while my mum is doing work outside for my dad. I put music on the tv and the kids are coloring. But I don't know why but I can't handle them all talking. It's really overwhelming. That's why I'm in my room a lot. Because all of them talking at once on top of the tv is too much for my head to handle. Some days I feel like my head will burst. My tiny head, tiny brain, consuming stuff that doesn't make sense, listening to all the noise. Hearing all the whispers in my ear from Al. My head will explode from being packed in with all this stuff. It hurts. Writing helps me deflate all the stuff in my head. I love that it does. Writing is kind of my thing. It just is. I have a problem, I write. I'm not a typical writer, writing books about fictional people. I am a storyteller though, but I don't tell other people's stories, I tell my own. I don't think I could write a whole book about fake people. I love reading one, but I could not do that myself. I can't write about stuff I don't know, if that makes any sense. I have to write about what I do know and what I know most about is my life. I don't know everything about my anxiety, but I'm willing to learn. I learn more about it everyday. I would say I learn more about myself too, but I don't. I'm a teenager so I don't really know who I am yet, I know what I like though so that helps. But I think in order for me to learn more about myself I have to let go of who I still think I am. When I think of myself, I think of a short annoying girl, with lots of baby chub, a high ponytail, and tries to dress & act like everyone else. She did what she thought would make her fit in. I'm a little different now. I don't care as much, I don't try to fit in. But the only way I see myself is the way I used to be. And I don't want that. I want to be the opposite. The way I want to see myself is the way I write about myself. That's who

I want to be. Just minus the anxiety. There's a quote I love by Dan Millman, "You don't have to control your thoughts. You just have to stop letting them control you." That's what I want. That's someone I want to become. I also feel like I feel things so hard. I feel too much. Like I just saw a video and it was a girl who got rejected for the way she looked, then she went home absolutely destroyed. I can't relate to her at all but I feel so much sympathy for her. I just watch it and instantly become my feelings. Just like my thoughts. I *become* my thoughts and feelings. I know it might sound weird but it's true. Whatever I'm feeling & thinking sets my mood, what I eat, say, watch on tv, everything. But one thing that doesn't depend on anyone else is giving up. Because giving up sounds really good right about now. I've never seen or watched anyone give up their life. But it seems appealing to me. Not doing anything. Laying in bed all day, not caring about school or hygiene, socializing, cleaning, eating. Seems like it's the only way I can get a break. So why not? Seems like the best option to me, mostly because I have no other options.

CHAPTER SIXTEEN
As of lately

I have tried so many times and so many different things to fix myself. Obviously none of them work. I would journal, eat healthy, workout, hangout with friends and still have to chill out and get my stuff done. Sounds really good right? But no. The workouts made me feel pathetic. Like I can't do as much as the girl in the video can or I don't look that way. Eating healthy is easy but takes more effort to make. Journaling wasn't your typical journaling thing, I'd basically write stuff that I knew I'd accomplish in the day so I could just feel the tiniest bit of pride in myself. I'd hangout with my friends too, that would be easy but so tiring. Getting my stuff and chores done was obviously easy, but again tiring. But the 'chill time' was basically me sitting and going on my phone or watching tv. I'd do all of this maybe one every 1-2 months and give up after a while because I wasn't any happier. I realized that no matter what I try to do to fix it, I can't. No matter how hard I try to get rid of Alastor, I can't. I used to wake up at 6:00 in the morning everyday in the summer to go on a run. I had so much gumption. Sadly I don't have that gumption for any else, but I just can't believe I did that. I think that it was mostly because it was the summertime and I'm always happier in the summer. And I was so hard on myself to do better, to reach my goal. And I'm super competitive with myself so obviously I did it. I want to do that again. I *want* to have that motivation, and want to do it in general. I haven't worked out in probably a month. Obviously I have gym class but that's nothing. And the reason I haven't is because I'm tired. I sound like a broken record at this point. I can just see myself slipping right back into my old patterns and my old ways. I'm home a day or two every week. I feel the same way I was last year. Two different people. One was school Maya, the other was home Maya. Very different people. I keep trying to hangout with friends and to socialize but they have lives, they're busy. And I can try to do a hobby or two but they only take up a few hours of the long day. Anxiety is like being tired and scared all at once. I heard that in a video before. And it's true. You're completely exhausted but totally terrified so you have to keep your eyes open. You want to fall asleep but you can't. And my anxiety gets the best of me when I'm not feeling well, physically. I'm getting over the stomach flu currently. I was nauseous and nauseous for hours until I finally threw up. I threw up twice total and I was crazy tired. I was sweating but freezing, and my legs were so achy. That was pretty much two days. All night Saturday I was nauseous, no sleep, & throwing up. Lucky if I got 2 hours of sleep. Sunday, I was so achy, absolutely exhausted, felt gross, and had a 6 hour nap. I slept the whole night though which was good. When I was feeling like this I got anxious thinking the feeling was never going to go away. I was going to feel like this forever and ever. Obviously I'm not feeling that way anymore, but it sucked. I thought that I'd become so sick that I'd have to be taken to the hospital and they'd diagnose me with some long lasting disease. Alastor puts some crazy scenarios in my head. Makes me think insane things. I know you're probably curious as to what Alastor even looks like. And I couldn't tell you because I don't even know. To me he's just mean, a bully. Someone who thinks they're so cool and always has a smug look on their face. He's tall, & big. Always looking down on me. He thinks he's above me, better than me. But I don't see him that way. He's the villain that you can never see the good in. He's not a human person to me. More of just a voice in my ear. Like a tiny person living in my head controlling things. When he talks I don't see him, I just hear him, and he's *so* loud. I want to be able to visualize him. But I can't. I also don't know why it's a *him* either. Probably because he's not mean like a girl. I've been bullied by both and it hurts more coming from guys. And the way Alastor treats me feels like that. I feel like it'd be easier to blame Alastor than to blame me, if Alastor had a face. Something to pin him to. A face to get angry at. But As a result of me slipping back into my old self and bad habits, I've started to think the same thoughts I did then. Death being one of them. Dying. Why it's such a sad thing? I think about the people I love not being with me anymore. Think about my animals not being here anymore. Me not being here anymore. Makes me sad. Because death is inevitable. It is going to come to us all one day. But I don't want to think about it, I want to live in the moment and not worry about it. But it just makes me so sad and so scared. Not for the actually dying part, I don't care about that. It's the fact that I'm not going to have everyone and everything I love anymore. It will be gone. That scares me. I don't want it all to be gone. I wish that 'forever' was real. Lately that's all

Alastor

I've been thinking about. Makes me tear up everywhere. On the bus, at school, in the living room, my bedroom. Why do I never stop thinking? Why did Alastor have to pull up an old fear from the past? I'm scared. I'm just scared of losing what I love. The people and animals I love. The home I love. Everything I love. It will all be gone. Thinking like this makes me hug my parents a little tighter & makes me grateful. I find that thinking like this makes me want to be with my parents 24/7. Like a kid. I feel the need to be with them all the time or know where they're going, where they will be. I get kind of clingy. And I don't know if they notice or not. But I don't care either way. I just like being with them. And my animals. I make sure I say goodbye, hi, or I love you, before I leave for school, when I get home, and before bed. Always.

I also often think about why Alastor chose me. Why did he pick me? What did I do to make him torture me. And I never come up with an answer because I don't think there is one. I'm kind of crazy. There's a scientific explanation for the anxiety I have. Mostly because it's just a chemical imbalance. But I pretend that it's this guy who lives in my head that I named Al. When you think of it that way I sound insane.

Like what am I doing? I'm arguing with myself. Not the guy in my head. Samantha, my counselor, says it's a good thing I named him, and talk to him. Almost like befriending the enemy. Keep your friends close but your enemies closer type thing. But the thing is, he's not actually there. He's not real. But he *feels* real. I don't know how to describe it. It's weird. But I can't help talking back to him. Well not talking, more like disagreeing and arguing. And I don't actually have any Enemies but I do have people that I don't like, or a stronger word, hate. But I would never wish Alastor on them. Never. He is a torturer, and makes you suffer internally. And it sucks. They don't know that I have an Alastor. And I'd like to keep it that way, because they could use it against me. I could just be paranoid, but I feel like they'd manipulate me with it.

It's the next day I'm on the bus home, it's 2:00 on the dot. I'm listening to Taylor swift (obviously) while the bus driver yells at the kids in the back. School is so much more draining than you'd think. It's a lot. And I can't believe I haven't thought about this but we have new restrictions coming after March break. Big ones. Masks are optional everywhere, and everything pretty much goes to how it was before covid. So that means school goes back to how it used to be. Lockers, hallways, 90 kids in a gym all at once, *no mask.* All of these scare me. I don't want people to see my face. It's a shield almost. I mean I'm definitely going to wear a mask in public, but I won't in gym, or at lunch, or outside. But I have no clue if I'm going to wear it full time or not. I mean I sick of them but am I brave enough? To be honest I'm just shocked. Beyond shocked that everything is going back to 'normal'. Seems crazy to me, I wouldn't have expected it. I'm also completely shocked that I haven't gotten covid. I've been *so* lucky so many times. 3 times I should've gotten it but I haven't. Same with my whole family. We've all been so lucky.

CHAPTER SEVENTEEN
March Break

Ila often talks about how our friend Ella can't joke with me too much. And it's joking like calling me stupid or an idiot with a blank expression on her face. And Alastor makes me think she actually means it. Alastor makes me think everything is true. My mum was angry that I wasn't going to school today. I understand why she's angry. But she doesn't understand me. And that's not her fault. This morning I thought our conversation was light hearted because I was filling it with sarcasm and jokes. But my mum wasn't taking it as a joke. She was getting angry that I wanted to stay home. She said, "between you and your brother, you guys are going to be the death of me." And my mind, the way my mind works, thinks that it's true. I started to get a little teary. But I just kept trying to remind myself that she said it out of anger, she didn't mean it, it's a saying, a lot of people say it but they don't mean it. Over and over in my head that's what I try to keep telling myself. At the same time Alastor is telling me the opposite. And I don't want people to think they need to be careful with their words around me. It's my problem and I have to fix it.

Anyways since I'm home, I'm officially on March break. Thank god. It couldn't come sooner. It's a much needed break. But only a week long, which I think is stupid. But this March break I want to be totally chill. I wanna hang out with my friends though. I normally never do anything for March break. Last year the only thing I did was chop all my hair off, and have a sleepover/shopping with a friend. All in the span of two days. The rest of the break was nothing. I want to hangout with my friends at least 2 times this break. And my Mom, Aunt, Nan, & I are all going to this really cute café. We're going to talk 'business' about this book and just hangout. I think that will be fun. The coffee absolutely sucks there but Ila told me they have good tea, so I'll have that when we go.

It's now Sunday, the 13th. Me, my mum, Aunt, & Nan all went to our business meeting/cafe outing. It was nice. I got

Alastor

some things figured out for Alastor, and I felt very businessy. After talking to my aunt I have a ton of ideas, and have more options I'm thinking of exploring.

But speaking of my nan and aunt, I don't think I talk about my extended family a lot. I don't feel I've mentioned my nan, but I've never gone into too much detail about her or my grandparents on my dad's side. My nan is my mom's mother, my poppy died before I was born, so I don't know much about him besides the good stories I hear. But anyways my nan is a funny lady. She's just naturally funny. She's also really fun to play games with. Almost every time I go for sleepovers we play a card game. And I remember when I was younger, we would color and do arts and crafts at her table. I remember admiring the way she could color in the lines, and the way her pictures were always so perfect. And when I think of my nan I think of the way that she smells, I know that might sound weird but it's true. She smells like perfume, a clean perfume and coffee. So you know I obviously like the way she smells. I think of Christmas and how we always spend it with her. I also think of all the pictures she has. All the memories in these books. I think of how comforting her apartment is. It smells like coffee and candles and it is always the perfect temperature, and it's cozy. My nan is a really comforting person too. So, that's why I think her place is so comforting. She is short I guess, compared to me. She also has short blonde hair.

I'll stick to my mom's side of the family to talk about my aunt. My aunt is a busy lady. She's also super smart. You can tell by just talking to her that she's smart. She's practical. She is always putting herself out there for me and my family. She's always giving. She cares about us so much and it shows. She likes to take me on Starbucks dates, and we just talk. I'm really grateful for my aunt, she's like a second mom. She wants to make sure that we're all good, that we're making smart decisions. She is the one helping with this, Alastor. She goes through and reads it and edits it. And I'm so thankful for that because I know how busy she is, so the fact that she's taking time to do that means a lot to me. She loves to work and I admire that, I want to love to work just like her. My aunt is also kind of short too. And has a dirty blonde/brownish hair color.

Now moving onto my dad's side of the family, my Dada and Dadi. My dad is from India & that means grandparents. My grandparents are probably the most selfless people I've ever met and will meet. They are always sending us food and always give me and my brother money, for no reason. All they do is give give give. I wish there was a way that I could do the same for them. They know I have knee problems, so they searched up recipes and exercises that would help and sent me the food and showed me the exercises. They notice when I don't look so good, or my parents or my brother don't look so good and want to do what they can to help. My Dada is so sweet and so unintentionally funny. Both me and my dad think he is cute. He's tall like my dad, slim and wears a turban most of the times I see him. My Dadi cares so much for us & she is beyond kind. She isn't short, she's somewhat medium height. She has long black hair and always wears these really pretty colorful clothes. They are just such good people. All I want is to give them what they give me.

My dad has two sisters but they don't live in Canada, I know them but not very well. They know me more than I know them. And same on my moms side, except for siblings. It's just her and my aunt, but I have a ton of great aunts and uncles that don't live close to us. And again I don't really know them because the majority of time I spent with them was way back when I was little.

I do have cousins on my dad's side that live in Canada. They are almost 30 and both super successful, I admire that. They're hard workers.

CHAPTER EIGHTEEN
Socializing

It's been a few days. Ila and Morgan are coming over, Ella was supposed to but she can't. Every time we hangout we always go out or have the night planned with stuff to do. But that's a lot and it's tiring. So today we're just going to hangout and chill. Do nothing. Which I think is good. We need a break. They're both coming in a little over an hour & currently I'm laying on my bed on my side, my hang curled close to my stomach typing on my phone. I have my big water bottle, like big. A 2 liter water bottle that is a peachy color, I named it Bertha. You're supposed to drink 2 liters everyday, so I'm trying to. It has encouraging comments on the side with the times you're supposed to drink the water at. I'm doing better than I thought I would. Anyways I'm also listening to music. I've been listening to music like crazy lately. I don't know why but every second I have free time I'm listening to music. I like it though. It's nice to listen to music.

My music is hitting hard, I love my playlists. I have 'Fave tunes' which is pretty self explanatory. I have 'concentration music' music I use to study, 'morning music' is what I listen to when I get ready In the morning. 'Workin tunes' I use when I'm cleaning or working out. I also have 'kinda sad ngl', 'hype music', 'party jams', & 'running music'. But those you kind of have an idea of what they're about. I listen to Fav toones & Morning music the most. They are filled with a lot of Taylor swift, Olivia Rodrigo, Tame impala, and a few random songs I've found. Music has been therapeutic lately.

It's a day later. Music has changed. I'm listening to the sadder stuff. The stuff that makes me cry harder than I already am. Like right now. I listen to my sad playlist and just cry. Sounds stupid right. Well I'm stupid so it fits. Lately I'm just feeling so worthless. Unwanted. Hated. I feel like I'm ugly, stupid, and annoying. Sad. I don't know what it's like to feel heartbroken but I feel like what I'm guessing it's like. I feel like every time I breathe In a sharp breath and let it out sharp, unnerving, endless. No relief. I feel stuck. I feel like Alastor keeps asking for more, wanting more. So I give and give him more. It feels like ripping my soul & heart out of my chest, handing it to

Alastor

him with my weak hand. I slouch over as I feel it leave. As I feel the emptiness. I curl up in the same spot, same position on my bed with my phone. Trying to hold back tears in case my parents walk in. Is every teenager going through this? I thought I was good at hiding it. Acting. But if they go through this too, god their good actors. Another thing I can't do. Another reason I'm belittled compared to others. I just don't compare that's the thing. I'm just not good at things. Simple as that. I've accepted it. I know I'll never be good enough. Or pretty enough, funny enough, cool enough, smart enough. I know. I'm aware. I envy people who aren't like me. I also wish I could stop feeling this way. Go back to moments when I was genuinely happy or having fun. I remember the moments, the feeling I had, head clear, smile on my face. But nothing lasts forever. And that feeling especially. That one goes more than it comes. Never seems to stick. I want to go back. Back to that feeling. The feeling of a little bit of relief. The feeling where everything *seems* good. Ila and Morgan did come over and I had fun, so much fun. But when the night started to come to an end the exhaustion level increased, and the gloom hit. Like I said nothing lasts forever, especially the good stuff. I went to the living room and my mum was there, I told her I was tired and instantly broke down in tears. Because I'm broken and there's nothing I can do about it. That's frustrating. I remember telling her I just want it to be fixed, I want it to stop. I want Alastor gone.

It's a few days later and Tonight I'm going out to dinner with Ella, Ila, & Morgan. Then we're going to Ella's house for a movie and a sleepover. I'm hoping I don't bring this negativity with me. I hope that I can pretend to be positive for it. It's longer than I normally hangout with them so we'll see. I'm so beyond grateful for them, they are the best friends I've ever had. I'm hoping we stay friends till we're adults. I hope we stay in contact at least. They can tell when I'm not feeling well, and I try to hide it but they know. I have a really hard time expressing my emotions. I hate expressing my emotions. All I feel is weak and pathetic. Why, though? Aren't you supposed to be strong if you express your feelings? Like isn't it good if you do? But how come I don't feel any better? And since I don't feel any better, my mum is going to talk to my doctor about switching medication & seeing Lisa more. All I want is to be better.

Alastor

Dinner was good, the sleepover was good. I had a lot of fun but I'm really tired. We were up till 4 in the morning. Which is *hours* later than when I normally go to bed, so obviously that was weird for me. I also woke up at 8 so I didn't have a lot of sleep. When I got up everyone else was asleep so I tried to fall back asleep, but I couldn't. So I sat in this short chair and scrolled on my phone for like two hours. I messaged my mom asking to pick me up early. There's no reason or something that happened. I just wanted to be home. I needed to be at home. So she picked me up early, I didn't tell my friends why I was getting picked up early just in case it would hurt their feelings, I told them I had to get ready for my interview. When I got home I ate a little bit then fell asleep for almost 3 hours. When I woke up I had to get ready for this interview. So I got dressed as professional as I can with the clothes I have and I made sure I had everything I needed so I was prepared. I'm pretty sure I've never mentioned this, but I really want a job. I've put out 5 resumes and heard nothing so having an interview was exciting. I want a job so I can buy all the things that are piling up in my online shopping carts, and to be able to work in a real job environment. I want to be able to earn money and be responsible with it. I also want a savings account, not for anything in general, maybe a car. Anyways as soon as dad got home we left, and I already had a good word in at this job because my dad knows the store front manager and she told the manager manager that they should hire me. So I was feeling kind of confident. I go in to ask for the manager, & I have to wait a little while but then the manager comes out with papers and a pen. He asked me a few questions and I was pretty happy with how I answered them. I think I sounded really put together. While he asked me questions I filled in the papers and I pretty much got hired on the spot. I was so happy. I'm obviously a bit nervous because it's new, and I don't have my mom or dad's hand to hold while doing it. But I'm excited. I think this will be good for me. Keep me busy. I'll be working a 4 hour shift for now, on the weekends. I start the weekend after this one. I've already done the calculations of what I'll be making with the deductions and everything and I'll be making pretty good money for a 15 year old. The first few paychecks I'll probably just spend, spend on the things I've been wanting. But after that I'll start a savings account and 15-20 percent of what I make will go there. My savings is most likely going to be for a car. I want a little white beetle. I still have almost two years until I can drive but that's my dream car right now. Eventually in the future I want to upgrade my car to a white keep, that will be my 'grown up' car. I want to be able to drive so badly. I'm pretty sure I'll be the designated driver for our friend group and I don't mind. I'll be getting my license first assuming I pass. But It'll be fun. If I don't buy my own car when I get my fulls I'll drive my dad's truck. Which is kind of funny, because it's me driving the big truck. But I think I'll look pretty cool driving it. One of the biggest reasons I want to drive is to be able to go wherever I want whenever I want. If I randomly want something from the grocery store or something I can go. Or I want fast food, I can just go. Or if I don't have a drive to my friend's house, I can just drive myself. Also the one thing I want to do the most when I get a car is to drive to McDonald's, get fries and ice cream, and scream and sing along to Taylor swift. That's all I want to do. I bet you the day I get my fulls you'll see me in the parking lot of McDonald's with T Swift blasting. Also having a job is good because I can pay for the gas myself, and don't have to worry about bumming some off of mum and dad. To conclude that, I'm really excited about the job and I really want to drive. I think it's good for me to start a job young, kind of get ahead of the game. Even though McDonald's isn't what I want to do as a career, the experience is still good. I'm also starting to think of a career change. But I'm honestly stuck, because I don't know. I'm in between being a forensic psychologist and a journalist. Two very different things, I know. I'm super interested in the criminology stuff, but will I be good at it? And I love writing and I think I'm decent at it, plus there's always room for improvement. So is journalism a better idea for me? But a forensic psychologist gets paid more and I want to be rich. But I also want to love my job and not be completely stressed out. Can you see my little dilemma? I don't know what I'll do, I think highschool might help with my decision. We'll see. Maybe I can be a journalist for crimes and stuff?

CHAPTER NINETEEN
It's been rough

I've been fighting a thought for a few days. Mostly because I don't want to admit that it's true. I was having an appointment with Samantha the other day and a thought just randomly popped in my head and I didn't like it. It was that Alastor isn't real, which I know is true he's not but, the thought was That he's not the one to blame. I am. I am Alastor. Well I'm Maya. But the thought was that I created this person to blame it on (Alastor), when really I'm the one to blame. I'm the one torturing myself or there's a different version of me hurting me. I want to take a little bit of pity on myself, or I want to think that I'm a good enough person to not do that. Even not to myself. But I can't help but think that it's not true. As much as I don't want Alastor, I'd rather him than me. I'd rather him hurting me than myself. But I just reassure myself that if I wanted it to go away, my anxiety. It would. Because I have control over myself, not Alastor. So if

I really wanted to get rid of it I could, but I'm not in control of it, yet. Alastor is. But I do often think of how much I see myself in Alastor. But that's because he feeds off of me. He was assembled in my brain, with all of my bad characteristics. You know how you have a devil and angel version of yourself on your shoulders, well if I had a devil Maya, Alastor is like the boy version. I'm hoping that soon I can get an angel one to tussle with Alastor for a bit, get him off my back. And even if I do get an angel one, I don't want the angel to beat Alastor. I want to be the one who wins. Me. I think I forget the science on my anxiety a lot and dive into my imagination with it. But it's so much harder for me to believe the scientific stuff because I don't understand it. So it's way easier for me to give in to the 'Alastor' of it all. This is kind of off topic but I feel almost heartbroken in a way. Because of Alastor, I've never been in a relationship before and I've never been broken up with, but I would definitely say that I've felt heartbroken, just not in that way. And I would say I'm heartbroken. Not sure why. Just feels like my heart is aching. Maybe it's just me feeling pitiful for myself, I don't know. But it sucks. Just feels like there's no point to anything at all. No reason for me to get out of bed in the morning. Almost like I broke up with being happy. But I didn't want to break up with happiness. I miss it. I also just feel so lonely. Very alone. And it's not like I want to be in a relationship or something, I just feel lonely. I want to be wanted. In any way. Because I feel so unwanted. Not by anyone in specific, just in general. And lately I just feel like if I feel any emotion, I have to turn it to anger. That might just be the teenager in me, but I don't know. I think that it's the frustration of it all. I feel like the only acceptable way to act with my emotions is by anger. You might think that I've been a hot head lately from reading that, but no. I kind of keep the anger and all my emotions in general, to myself. Mental health has become a pretty big topic, it used to not be. I once read an article that people in psychiatric care had less anxiety than highschool kids do today. That's crazy. Mental health is something that is a touchy subject. I think that people should talk openly about it if they're comfortable doing so. It needs to be made into something that is normalized. But if I ever did that people would think that I belong in a mental institution. Kids these days don't realize how normal being depressed and anxious is. Obviously it's not a good normal, but sadly so many people struggle with it. I do. And I hate it. Why can't I stand up in front of my class to give a 2 minute presentation?

Doesn't sound too hard? And when will I be able to forgive myself? Forgive myself for feeling normal emotions just 10 more than others. Forgive myself for the chemical imbalance in my head that I have no control over. when? I hold a lot of grudges but the biggest grudge I hold is on myself.

Everything would be so much easier if I were a kid again. Carefree, simple. Nothing mattered, the scariest things were the dark and monsters under your bed. What sucks is as you grow up, so do the monsters that hide under your bed. They grow up with you. But just like things change as you grow older, the monsters grow bigger & scarier. The dark you were afraid of gets darker. Some learn to live with it, or overcome it. Some don't. I didn't. I wish I could just tell myself when I was younger to just stay the same. Don't grow up because It's not fun. Wish I could at least tell her that it's scary, prepare yourself. I was thrown into a world that made me dreary & terrified. I wish I could give her a hug. Because I miss her. It's almost like I put sunglasses on. I used to see everything, the good stuff, how sunny it was. But now I'm older and I have sunglasses on. It's darker, scary, no good stuff to be found. But I know it's there, the sun, all happy things. I just can't see it. And I know everyone around me wants what's best for me, & to help me, but they don't. I just wish they would just give me a break. Let me breathe. I think they just don't realize how much I am trying, & the best I can do is how I'm doing now. I am doing the best I can right now, and I need that to be enough for everyone. I've always been there for myself, I can count on myself. Always. And I don't think I give myself enough credit for that.

I stayed home from school today. Going back after March break is so hard. I fell asleep this afternoon, then again, I just woke up from my second nap. It's 5:03. I didn't wake up by myself. My mum woke me up by saying, "Maya, Maya, wake up you already slept this afternoon, you're not going to sleep tonight." So I'm awake now. In between Cornelius's legs, my bear. I'm crying. Not sure why. I've been crying a lot lately. I think it's the frustration, because I can't fix it. I just feel like screaming. I don't want to go to my mom because she'll get angry. Probably say, "Maya you've missed way too much school already" or "You can't keep doing this" When in reality I'm not doing this. Because if I was I would be going to school no problem. I wish I was like the other kids, I wish

I had the willpower in myself to go to school everyday, I wish I was stronger like the other kids. The kids who deal with the same stuff but can still handle school on top of it. I *wish* I could do that. So badly. But I can't. I know I can't. I don't need to be reminded of it everyday. Even if it's in a joking way. Haha so funny that I find it hard to go to school. Maya is home more than she's at school. Pathetic. Why? What's wrong with me? Why do I find it so hard? Seems easy enough, so what's the issue?

"Maya you *have* to go to school tomorrow" I know, "you know that? You realize that?" Yes I know. As soon as she left my doorway tears rolled down my face. God I feel so weak. I don't want to disappoint her, I really don't. But that's all I feel like I'm doing right now. You know I've heard people say that people find comfort in their pain, & I never understood it until now. I find comfort in the feeling that I experience the most. It's not exactly pain though. Just Alastor. Alastor tricked me into thinking he was good. Warning me. Making me panic, so I'm safe. But Lisa told me that I basically have a big red button in my brain and it goes off when I'm in danger, but Alastor is pushing it all the time. Made me think he was keeping me safe, but he never was. And if Alastor hates me so much why does he stay? He pushes my buttons, literally. But he doesn't need to stay, so why? And if I wanted to change myself or change everything I do to get rid of him I can *never* go back to who I was before. That was my home. My old self was my rock. So as much as I change myself I can never go back to who I once was, I'll never be the same.

CHAPTER TWENTY
Life sucks

Every time you go to a mental health clinic or maybe on the phone with someone for mental health, one of the very first things they ask you is of your suicidal, or going to harm your self or others. Even if someone is, they'd never say it. I'm not. But at an appointment I had with Samantha the other day, we were just talking and she asked me if I was getting suicidal. I was a bit shocked. I didn't realize the words coming out of my mouth were bad enough for her to think that. I know she's just making sure and everything, which I'm thankful for. But Suicide makes me sad. Anytime I think of someone hating being alive or dealing with life or people so they kill themselves to get away from it. That breaks my heart. People don't feel like they have anyone to go to because they think they are alone. To them it's the only way out. It's horrible. I never knew self harm was a thing until middle school. Heard kids talking about how they cut themselves and thought it was cool. Looking back I didn't understand at the time, but now I'm disgusted. After that I never thought much of self harm. Sometimes in my brain when I am in the shower and see the razor, I never think of harming myself. I think of what *if* I did. Then immediately I tell myself, "why would you even think that '' or just shocked that I thought of it. But again it's not to harm myself, it's impulsive thinking. Just crazy bizarre thoughts that pop in my head. Because I know I would never, I'd never want to put myself in pain. Suicide on the other hand, I don't remember how long I've known about suicide. But, I know I've always felt the same way about it. It's sad. The thing with me is that I *want* to live. Because right now I'm not living. And me committing would defeat the whole purpose of what I want. I want to live, I want to love life. But I don't. Suicide wouldn't fix that. But, I have thought about it. Not in the sense of killing myself, more in a way of what people would think, and who would be sad, what would happen. And I think of what I'd leave as an explanation, or why I'd do it. But it makes me upset to just think about it. I don't like thinking about it. I haven't given up my fight against Al yet and me giving up would not be suicide. Killing myself wouldn't kill Al. So yes I'd give up on life, but not in that way. I'd just be super depressed and lazy & careless. That's how I'd give up. People commit suicide for many different reasons, mostly personal reasons. Like bullying, rape, assault, school, home life, drugs, depression, anxiety, ocd, ptsd, & many more mental illnesses. So many different reasons. So many. And it's horrible that these things can lead people to that. And it's horrible that the world and life failed them. They thought hope failed them. Which in a sense it did, hope just couldn't save them fast enough. Those people who the world lost to suicide were probably some of the strongest people out there, they were just too tired. And I wish they would have still been here today.

Rape is also a big reason for suicide. It absolutely disgusts me to think that people would do something so sick. To touch another person without consent. It makes you disappointed in the human race. It's so sad. I feel so sorry for the people that feel like they can't wash off the touch of a person. It's a horrible feeling being used. I honestly don't have much other to say besides it's sickening and I'm sorry.

Addiction, addiction is a pain. Something you think is good, something that makes you 'happy'. Addiction is a cruel thing to have. Because you think it helps, makes you happy, and makes you feel better. It's false hope. And that false hope is hard to let go of. Once you're addicted to something it probably feels impossible to get off of it. But it's not. I wish there's something I could do for everyone who has an addiction, but I have no clue, I don't know what words I could give. Besides, keep going, keep trying. Even when you feel like there's no hope.

I feel really strongly about the things I've said here. They are serious topics I don't think are discussed enough, there needs to be more awareness spread about them. And I know that these are sensitive topics but they do need to be addressed, in any way possible. Talking about it, not normalizing it because it's not normal to be raped, addicted to things, or so depressed you feel like you should hurt yourself or die. People who have to go through those things need help & support. They do not need to be criticized or made fun of for something they can not or could not control. They didn't or don't deserve it.

Alastor

I am no expert whatsoever with any of these topics, I have very little personal experience with them. What I've said here is from my perspective as a teen, also my thoughts and opinions on it. But please if you need help call your local crisis line.

The world we live in kind of sucks. I wish we all were kids again when everything was easier, better. We were clueless to all the bad things & everything seemed good. But no, if we were kids again we wouldn't even be thinking about these things, because then they didn't exist to us.

CHAPTER TWENTY ONE
Employed

It was my first day today. Working at McDonald's. I woke up at 5 and was there by 6. It was really weird at first. I was so anxious & so nervous. When the workers were showing me stuff and how to do things I felt completely stupid, because I didn't know what I was doing. And yeah I know it's my first day. I keep trying to remind myself of that. I felt like THEY thought I was stupid or annoying or incompetent. They probably didn't but I just felt like they were annoyed with me. But once my real trainer got there, who I know, it got a bit easier. It was also easier when it got a bit busier. I don't know why. But it was just easier. I was too busy to think. It also helped that I was kind of getting the hand of the cash register. The majority of the customers understood I was in the process of being trained but a couple didn't and were kind of impatient, which was expected. But the job itself isn't too hard once I'm fully trained it'll be even better. It's kind of the fact that it's new, I don't know the people I'm working with, I don't know how the customers will act if I slip up a little, or how my co workers will be if I do. I feel alone. Exposed almost. That's what scares me, not the job. I was actually shaking. Like really bad. I thought my co-workers were going to see, but they didn't thank god. They'd tell me to put a jacket on or something. When in reality I was shaking from anxiety. My whole body was shaking. I thought I might fall or stumble because it was so bad. I also kept getting anxiety shivers. But the worst part is now over. No introductions, no one telling me HOW things work more so showing me or helping me to do it better. No more getting my uniform, because I now have it. I also look pretty good in the visor not gonna lie. And no more tours of the place. Shouldn't be as scary tomorrow. Obviously I'm still going to be nervous again and probably will be every time I work. But, it will soon be just like school. I'm nervous at school all day everyday, so work will be like that too. Except I get paid :) motivation for work won't be hard. Especially since it's actually kind of fun when you get into a groove doing it, and money. School I see no reason to go to. Nothing at school benefits me or gives me anything. I don't get paid to go to school, I don't actually learn anything. All they teach you is how to read and recite. Boring to me. Seeing my friends is good but I can see them on weekends so I'm good with that. Anyways, the first day at work was okay. I give it a 6 or 7 out of 10.

I rate the whole day, a 5/10. Later it was Ilas' birthday. We went to her house dressed all cute, opened presents, ate pizza, and just hung out. I was having a lot of fun. We later went downtown, tried to find some stores to shop at that were open, but most of them were closed. I did do a little shopping though which was fun. At around 7:00 we went to a place to get dessert, we ordered, we ate, it was good. We were all having a lot of fun and completely stuffed full. But then the check came and I wanted to get rid of my cash and just pay the rest on debit. So I asked and they said I could. So I got the machine and I didn't know how to work it. They were all at one saying different things to me, but even though they weren't that loud they sounded like they were yelling in my ears. I kept messing up and the waiter looked annoyed and gave it back, and I messed up the payment even though I got it done, and paid I forgot to tip. So, I felt super bad because I was being a hassle and I didn't even tip. My friends looked at me in a way I don't really know how to describe but it wasn't a good way. I felt stupid, annoying, & embarrassed. It was so hard with them all (to me sounded like) shouting at me. At the end before we left, they said that I was being complicated and I shouldn't have done it. Then I was like sorry I didn't want cash. I didn't know it was going to be difficult like that. But then I was like I'm going to have a panic attack. And I did. I was red, shaking, and tears rolled down my face. Then they all felt bad. And I just tried to play it off cool by making a joke of it and acting funny, but it wasn't. I didn't feel funny. They kept me somewhat distracted, so it wasn't hard to get over the attack. But later we were walking down to the waterfront and this homeless man asked for money. And I said back, "what did you say" and they all whispered at me "maya no!" "Maya keep walking" and stuff like that as they pushed me to keep walking and ignore him. My parents didn't raise me like that. I know my friends were just thinking the worst. Like he wanted to kidnap or hurt us, or he was on drugs or something, but he looked like a regular homeless man to me. But then they just said it was stupid of me to do that and that's not smart, you never do that. But my parents told me later to not think about it because they would have done the same thing. But it really wasn't nice to hear, keep getting nagged at about how bad your mistakes are. It hurt. Especially coming from my friends. I know they were just worried, and they have every right to be. It's not their fault at all, but I don't think it's mine either. But I'm still upset about it. It didn't feel good. So for the rest of the night I was quiet. They asked if I was okay. I wasn't. Then we went back to Ilas house and I was quiet the whole ride there. My mum was there not long after and she dropped off Morgan first then we went home. I messaged her prior telling her I had a panic attack. So she asked what happened and stuff and I told her and broke down. Then I broke down again while my mum helped me tell my dad. But to be honest I think I'm just really tired, and overwhelmed.

I had my second day of work. It was longer than my first day, I did 6-2 today. Wasn't that good. All I could think about was when it was going to end. I had a better trainer but that's pretty much the only good thing. I feel so useless and stupid. Not knowing what I'm doing, how to do everything. All I think about is every single mistake I made or every time I messed up. I couldn't sleep thinking about it all. I think my anxiety makes it worse though. I think that's the reason I'm so overwhelmed. I didn't realize how fast everything really is. My trainer said it will take me months to be able to get used to it. That leaves me so doubtful of myself. My parents think I should try it out again for next weekend and if I still feel the same I should quit. They don't want me to give up that easily but I know myself better than anyone and I know what I can and can't handle. I'm so close to having a mental breakdown because of it all. I am still pretty young anyways so I don't need or have to get a job. I just wanted the experience and the money. So if I still have this put in my stomach next Sunday I'll be quitting and my plans for shopping and stuff will go in the trash. I have to find another way to make money from now until I turn 16. When I can work a slower job, something not too stressful for me. But we will see. I just really want all this to end. Alastor. I want him to end. It's so disappointing because I really wanted this job. I was so excited, too excited I guess.

I didn't quit, it just took me time to get used to it. It's good now. I haven't written in awhile, trying to hold off. I'm ahead of where I'm supposed to be in this, not too far ahead only like a month. Because I'm supposed to write about school ending soon & summer. It's April 5th. I have three months to go. But I'll still write about it. I can't wait for summer, I have big plans. I feel like this summer is going to be the best one yet. All the stuff I want to do is very reasonable, I can do most of it myself, some with my parents, some with friends. This summer WILL be good, I'm determined. School can't be over quick enough. I'm getting so sick of it. Saying goodbye to the place I hate the most. It'll be a happy relief. I'll probably be wishing I burned the place down when I got the chance or something like that. Middle school sucks. I loved elementary school, hated middle school, hope to love high school and university. We will see. High school seems to be better anyways. You get to have some choice of what courses you take, I love a lot of the electives I chose. They appeal to my interests. But I have to wait till grade 12 for my favorite ones like journalism, sociology, and law. They all seem really fun. But I'm hoping things will be different for me in highschool, I'll think differently and stuff. Be better. Highschool is a whole different dynamic and atmosphere so hopefully that difference and change will do me good. It's actually hard to imagine leaving the school that's held on to me so tight. Hurt me so badly. It's like leaving a toxic relationship. I'm excited to get rid of it. Never see it again. And summer, summer sounds like heaven right now. I think summer will be so good just because of how rough this year has been. Everyone is anticipating summer I think. But I want my summer to be filled with hanging out with my friends and family, working and making money, staying off my phone as much as possible, & checking everything off my summer bucket list. I want this summer to be one to remember, lots of laughing so hard you almost pee yourself. The naps you take after being out all day swimming. And the tans you get even when you wear sunscreen. The walks you take with your friends while eating ice cream. Family dinners outside because it's so nice. Ugh, I can't wait.

CHAPTER TWENTY TWO
No progress

Lately I've been feeling like our friend group isn't doing well. And that's only my view of it because we all play different positions. But we're not really a group anymore and I don't like it. I feel like I'm drifting away or pushing them away. Because I have to ruin all good things going for me. I don't want them to be a face you see in the hall and just smile at. That's not at all what I want. I want us to be close next year. Not close knit besties, but still close. I also saw a video on my phone of Ila and Ella hanging out. My heart dropped to my stomach. I was so angry, where is Morgan? And I think I was taking my feelings from us not being a group onto that. I don't care if they hang out with just the two of them. Who cares? It's kinda the fact that it was three of them and it seemed like Morgan was singled out. She was left out purposely. I completely jumped to conclusions and assumed when I shouldn't have. But me admitting that is actually pretty big of me because I never think I'm wrong. But Morgan was a close contact so she couldn't go. I told Ila and Morgan. Morgan felt horrible. And Ila was happy I told her, it's good to talk about something in the group that's bothering me. Because lately Ella only wants to hangout with Ila and sure I get it, but you know we are a friend *group*. And I miss it. The group. But when me and Ila were talking about it there was a lot of miscommunication. And I was so confused with half the stuff she was saying and she was not happy with things I said. But of course the stuff she wasn't happy about, wasn't what I meant. She thought I meant I didn't want us hanging out by themselves, just two of them. But I don't care. What I care about is if there are only 3 people and 1 is left out it *seems* like that one person is excluded. Which is what I thought happened. But it didn't. And the stuff Ila *thought* I said hurt her feelings but that stuff I said wasn't what I meant, so I felt really bad. It was a mess. The whole thing. Until we got to the end and actually understood what we were saying. Everything is fine. But you probably thought my friend group was perfect didn't you. The way I talk about it makes it sound like it. But nothing is perfect including us, but I would like to say my friend group is pretty close to perfect. Just short of it. We normally never have problems, ever. And to be honest this wasn't a 'fight' it was just a very messy conversation of how I've been feeling lately. I'm surprised I actually told them how I was feeling. Because there was a really good chance I could have messed it all up. I just remember crying at night thinking I wasn't going to have friends anymore. That I *didn't* have friends anymore. I was grieving over something that hadn't even ended. I have more hope now, for our friendship.

And the reason I still have hope is because I can tell them about my bad days. Like today. Today sucked. I worked today. My 6th day. It was fine, boring. Until the manager yelled at me and this random girl for talking. Yelled at us to work when I'd already done all the things they've taught me. Then my manager put me in drive through window 1. I was barely shown how to do it, but I did it anyway, it got easier. Then I went to break. Break was 30 minutes. I come back from break and the lobby is full. I normally don't cuss but I since I'm writing this it doesn't count. It was a complete shit show. We are normally never busy. I was put on the counter, alone. I had to take like 15 customers orders and then make their 15 drinks. All by myself. And I need a code or help or something

I can't even remember and I was waiting, the customer was waiting for the other manager to come help me. I could tell the customers had some sympathy for me which was nice at least. Drink station, a mess. Coffee on the floor, counter, everywhere. I was shaking like crazy. My legs were wobbly and I couldn't do anything with my hands and not spill a little. One of the crew members was being nice trying to stay calm, probably to get me to be calm. She told me not to worry about the mess, take care of customers, it's ok. That made me feel a little better. Then, I was told to get cream from the back. I know where it is, I've gotten it before. I go, and the door is blocked with these big heavy boxes that my noodle arms couldn't lift. And the same manager that yelled at me came to the back. She saw me looking around and yelled that the fridge is here. In my head I was like no duh, I'm looking for something to do with the boxes. Then she kept saying it's in the cooler. What's cooler? She moves the boxes, opens the fridge, gets what she wants. I'm looking around cluelessly for a cooler and she yells at me again saying "it's right there! You've been here 3 weeks and you don't know where anything is?" I just didn't say anything back. I got that bad pit in my stomach. She left and I just picked up the cream and brought it out. I was near tears but I held them back at least until I was off. I was so angry. I was angry at her. A cooler is something that is small, normally blue, and you bring it camping or to the beach to keep your food cold. A fridge on the other hand is a fridge. A fridge with a bag of cream in it. You know if you're going to speak English, speak it right. Or at least in a way I'll understand. Also I was angry at the fact that she said I was here for three weeks and I didn't know where things were. That's a big exaggeration. I've been working six days in a very badly organized fast food restaurant and was never fully trained. Also no offense to her but she is a grown woman and she makes a living at McDonald's. She is not one to judge. Anyways at 11 I told her I was off and she asked if I wanted to stay. I said I can't. My mum was there and I already punched out. But obviously I didn't want to. I got to the car still on the brink of tears and my mum asked what's wrong and I got so frustrated again. My mum felt horrible. And she understands why I didn't talk back to her. Because I have really bad anxiety which is pretty clear I think. Anyways I cried in the car, I stopped crying then got home, cried some more. And my dad was so angry. He was about to shut down that McDonald's. They asked me if I wanted to quit. I said no. Because it was one day. It can get better. But if it gets worse, I can't mentally deal with it. The work itself is fine. The judgment, not okay. I'm too fragile In the head. I'm going to keep going. But if it doesn't get easier or better for me, there's also a really good chance it could get worse. And if it does, looks like I'll be looking for a different job. Or maybe a break from a job, chill. But that means my huge shopping list will be on hold. I don't like the thought of that. Sorry for that long spiel but I told my friends. Not as detailed but they felt bad. Made me feel a bit better. Also me and my mum watched the triplets. The Sturnilolo Triplets. They are so funny. I always watch them when I want to laugh or feel sad and want to cheer up. I love them, they make me laugh so hard my stomach hurts. Or they just can be relatable. They're only 18 so they're not that old but they seem so grown up in the most immature way. It's the best. They can be deep and realistic but I like to watch them to get away from that stuff. There's Nick, Chris and Matt. I love them all but visually Matt is my favorite. Ila and Ella watch them too. Ila likes Chris the most so it works out perfectly. Ella can't decide so she chooses all of them. Morgan says they are too chaotic for her which is understandable but I find that hard to see myself. They seem like really good people, good guys. They just hit 1 million subscribers which is amazing. They deserve it. I've always thought of what it would be like to be famous. Seems cool but also terrifying. People are always watching you, being rude to you. That's scary. Especially for me. My anxiety would not be able to handle it. At all. I would be in a nervous breakdown the whole time. I'd fall off the face of the earth just to escape it. I have TikTok. I have my regular account which is private. Then I have my friends account, which I thought was private. It wasn't. I posted a video I thought only my friends would see. It was a video about me missing so much school. It was supposed to be funny. It was supposed to be a joke. Since it's only a friend's account, I only get 10 likes per video. I got almost 60 likes, 20, comments, 2, shares. The comments were horrible. Saying that "it's not a flex" I know, I wish I could go to school like everyone else does. Or "I hope you fail & live on the streets, seems like that's where you're heading" Gee thanks. "homegirl is 12 flexing her ditching school" I'm not ditching, I'm mentally Ill and can't handle it. "Embarrassing" I know right? I can't go to school like every other kid can? Pathetic. "It's not worth it" no duh. "Just go to class" would if I could. These are all the things I want to say to these random people who don't know me and don't know what I go through. But I reframe, I don't want to feed into it. I want to be a bigger person. But to be a little bit petty I liked all of the comments so they know I saw it. And Let them think I don't care. I hate that that's what being "famous" is like. Why would anyone want that? I feel horrible for the triplets if they have to deal with any of that. These people don't know me. But yet, they judge me & criticize me. I immediately turned my account private. I turned the video private too, just because. I was angry. Angry at these people for assuming. I was also freaked out. Because of course Alastor ate all this up. He loved it. Loved that random people on the internet were rude to me. Awe poor Maya, is she getting bullied? So vulnerable. Oh well, anyways. That's definitely what he's thinking. I want to know what he will be thinking when this book is done and out. I'm the world. He's exposed. But again so am I. But not in a bad way. I wonder if he will feel the tiniest bit defeated. It's going to take me so much work, time, & effort to get this out there. So much. I have it all planned out. I want this book done in 4 months. Which is totally doable for writing, that'll be easy. However. It's going to be pricey. I'm 15 and I do not have a ton of money. So I've decided to start working 8 hour shifts if I can, starting May. I'll work 2 days a week, maybe more in the summer. It's definitely pretty expensive to self publish, but I own everything. It's all mine. Which I like. I'm thinking about everything. Thank you gifts to those who helped, a launch or 'I did it' party. And the book's not even done yet. Clearly, because you're still reading. I'm just so excited. I want people to read it. I want people to feel comfort in this. I'm beyond excited and proud of how far I've come with this. If something doesn't work out or I realize how bad this is I will be heartbroken. This has been one thing I can rely on, and it will always be there. I know that I personally can do everything myself. I can work and make money, I can write better, fix all the mistakes, I can do it. I just need to know that it will happen. I feel so doubtful about myself. I *want* to believe I'm good enough to do it. Because I've become so determined and am anticipating the day I can share this with the people who need it. I just need support. Support from those around me. And, obviously support from people donating money to this. I hope people will. I want this out to people so bad. I want it to help people. Not being well mentally affects everything. Your physical health, school work. Social life. Everything. It messes you up. It's such a dark and scary thing. It's literally a monster in your head. And people think it's them. Which it is kind of. But it's not *you*. You would never do that to yourself. Because you're good enough to know you deserve better. It's a messed up different version of yourself. A mindset that feels inescapable. Like you're a prisoner in your own mind. Always regretting things you wish you did, wish you said. So many thoughts and opinions you hold in because you're scared of the backlash. Insisting to not give up when your own mind has broken you down. Telling yourself "you're going to do it. You've got this. It's okay. You're okay". But not feeling confident in those words. You want to live, not just survive. You want more than just existing. You want to be the main character of the stories that will be told. You don't want to be forgotten. You always feel like something is missing. Missing in your life. You wish you were still happy. Back when you still cared. You're too scared to burn bridges that aren't steady anymore. Scared of the outcome. People always tell you "you aren't going through this for nothing". So did we deserve it? Deserve to feel like this? "It will make you stronger". Stronger than I am now? All the time it feels like everyone thinks I'm not strong enough, tough enough. So sensitive. I feel like I'm pretty damn strong. I always do until someone says something. "I want you to be strong". You don't think I am? Feels like I'm never doing enough for anybody. I'm not tough enough for my parents, too emotional. Not good enough for my friends. Being in groups sucks because I am unable to present with them. Going through what I do all day everyday makes me think I'm pretty durable. But *everyone* makes me feel weak. Pathetically sad. Not like it's intentional but it still happens. Trying is never enough for anyone. Even if you're trying your absolute best. Your absolute hardest. It's the kind of frustration you get when your music can't go any louder. Not loud enough to block out the thoughts. It's annoying. But the feeling when the music is actually loud enough is amazing. It feels like you can breathe. Breathe big steady breaths. Makes you feel the tiniest bit of relief and contentment. Mental health issues suck. You always know when you're getting bad again. Almost like you find comfort in it. I always try to check in with my friends when I'm not completely distracted by myself. Make sure they are doing okay. I always put on a front for them, I don't want them to think of me as weak or fragile. I don't really want them to check in on me. I want to be alone. Do it myself. Same with getting better I don't want to have to talk to people or be on medication. I want to do it myself, and get better by myself. But I know that it's not possible. I can't do it alone. Neither can you, you need help, support, and to not be alone. Being alone is definitely not the best option. Taking care of yourself is also so hard sometimes. Feels impossible. Mental illness looks so different and can be different for everyone. It probably is mostly different for everyone. Some people have triggers. And some people don't. I do. Talk about death, dying. In any way it triggers me. I don't know why. Because I'm not afraid of dying, I'm afraid of not living my life now. Not being mentally well changes you. Completely. Turns you into a person you don't even recognize. A stranger. You know the saying, people can come in all shapes and sizes. Well it's the same with being mentally ill. Like I can't wait for the day I don't have to wear my fidget ring when going out. Or being nervous about posting a picture or a video on social media. When will that be? I find myself often longing for the feeling of being better. Waiting. I feel like I've been patient enough haven't I? Everyday, getting up, going to school, doing my work, just being there is so hard. I also have to deal with the assholes in my class. I know I'm sorry for swearing but I don't care, I'm just so angry. They think they are the coolest people there, think they are so funny for making rude jokes that might hurt people's feelings. Like one time they said something to Ila. That made me angry. They think that they have a right to be rude and I mean comments about other people, the things they do, what they look like, what they wear. Like can you just mind your business? But what I find funny is that they think people care. They have said many things to me before, many times. But I just don't care. Like it's sad. To think that being a shitty person to people makes them feel better about themselves. Some people would say they were jealous, which could also be true. Also the fact that they all go on about the alcohol and the drugs they did at that 'sick' party they went to on the weekend. But good for them. I'm happy for them. I'm happy they think it's good to post it all on social media, so that way all the stupid things they've done are out there forever. Congratulations. If that's what they want then great. See my brother does what they do, exactly what they do. I've learned from second hand experience. He did it because he's not a leader, he's a follower. He sees one of his friends doing it, he's going to do it too. It's just the way it is. It's sad. But I feel sorry for those people. Sucks for them. They like to go on about how I go to bed early and don't have a social life. And that's okay. If they want to think that it's fine by me. At least I'm not known for how drunk I can get or how I know where to buy the good weed. There's nothing wrong with smoking weed or drinking. Nothing. Just don't show it off or exaggerate it on social media. Not the best way to build a reputation. And do it in moderation. Not in the school washrooms every day every class. I know I seem like a really degrading person about myself, which I am. But I compare myself to these kids and I do think I'm better than them. Smarter. Because there being stupid. And I think I have every right to think I'm better than them. Sounds super self centered I know. But if I only hangout and go out to do things once or not every week, go to bed early, am not 'cool' I don't care. Think what you want of me, I could care less. You do you, just don't think you have any right to be judging others. I'm just so tired. Tired of people, work, trying. It took me a half hour to get out of bed this morning. 30 whole minutes. I went to bed around 9, got a good sleep, yet I'm so exhausted. I physically could not get up. My eyelids so heavy, my body not wanting to move. My alarm was going on and on so loud but I could care less. Least of my concerns. I was fine sleeping with it on. That can't be healthy?

CHAPTER TWENTY THREE
Lots of thoughts

I'm at school right now, I kind of have a free class so I decided to write to you. I'm listening to music, hoping my airpods won't give out and it'll blast my Taylor Swift playlist to the class. I probably should be doing the work I haven't finished but I'm completely unmotivated to do that. Or anything at all. You guys are the only thing that motivates me these days. Working for you, working to get this out there. I have an old black folder I keep all my plans, contacts, information, financial stuff, and just paper work in general in. Stuff to help publishing and working easier. I'm actually quite excited, I have a consultation today with someone from a publishing company. This is one of the only things that make me happy these days. Getting this out there, helping people, knowing I did it. I've got everything planned out. I'm just waiting for someone who knows how to write a book to read it. I'm hoping the suggestions are only minor, or not related to my writing itself. He's a busy guy, a friend of my aunts. I'm just hoping that I still have all this excitement when he gets back to me. I feel super businessy though, very professional, put together. It's kind of funny, but it's true. Like today I have a consultation, then I have another one right after school tomorrow with a different company. I'm just trying to feel out the whole publishing thing, see what place is best for me. I also wrote a list of questions for both appointments, just so i'm prepared and not completely blanking on what to talk and ask about on the call. I'm surprised to say I'm not nervous, just excited. I also planned everything I want to do every step of the way so I have an idea of what I'm doing. So for example my advertising and marketing im asking ms C and ms G if they can share my go fund me, Ms C already said yes. I haven't talked to Ms G yet.

I never thought I would ever feel this way. Ever. Last night, I had a panic attack. Regular panic attack. Then I got in the shower and sobbed. Partly because of the panic attack and partly because I'm just so emotionally exhausted. I had to sit down. I just sat down. I wasn't even thinking and I just sat down. I closed my eyes because I was just so tired. And the

Alastor

sound of the water hitting the tub was soothing. I sat there for probably about 15 minutes. After I got out of the shower I just went to my room and laid down. I fell asleep. I hadn't made my lunch yet, or done my homework or set my alarm. I was totally unprepared, but I slept the whole night, right into the morning. My mum was angry, upset. Understandable. But I tried to explain to her not long after what it's feeling like but she was angry just because she was having a bad day. I get it. It's okay. I messaged her this after,

"I'm sorry that you feel that way and I understand that you have bad days everyone does but it's like that for me everyday I'm on the brink of tears everyday. You're not a bad parent you and dad just don't understand. You guys think I'm fine when I'm not. It's so hard and I'm trying so hard and I don't think you guys realize that. I'm lucky that you guys are good with my anxiety but sometimes it's really annoying when you don't know the extent of it. I want to be Better, I want to be able to go to school and I beat myself up about it. Hearing it again from you and dad doesn't help. I could stop trying so hard but I try for you guys because I don't want to disappoint you but that's all I feel like I'm doing. I know you guys are sick of me being this way but I am too, I have to deal with it first hand and it just feels unfair. Words can't describe how hard I'm trying and how unbearable it is. I'm sorry you guys have to deal with me being the way I am. School is the least of my concerns, more so keeping it together and not completely falling apart. My book is one of the only things keeping me going right now, it's the only thing that's helping but it's still not enough. I'm sorry. And I'm sorry you're not having a good day."

She apologized she didn't need to but she did. Anyways I went to walk copper and I put my AirPods in and while I was walking him I was so upset that I thought something. Something I never thought I'd think about. I'm crying writing this because it breaks my heart. I was listening to music and my eyes filled with tears. And I thought, things would be easier if I weren't alive. And I didn't disagree with myself. Maybe things would be easier for those around me. And maybe I will finally be able to rest. Everything would be quiet. Alastor would be gone but so would I. I'm tired of wanting to be happy, I'm tired of trying, I'm tired of wanting to live life. I'm just done. I'm tired of being put through this everyday. I've held on for so long but I'm tired of holding on. When will things get better? Every breath I take I expect to make me feel better. But I end up hyperventilating, taking big breaths really fast in and out but air not actually coming in. I'm always going to try to make a joke out of it. Isn't it funny that right before I thought about it I was picking up dog shat? I think that's just a little funny. I'm not going to try anything, because I still don't want to die. But I also don't feel like being alive. But that doesn't mean I'm not going to think of it. God my head hurts. It feels tight. Like it's jammed packed with all these thoughts. The pills I take don't help. I take them with coffee. Not water. Coffee. I hate how I still feel the same. My meds aren't doing anything. Feels like I'm in the water and every time I try to come up for air, a wave comes crashing down on me. Then I'm right back where I started. Trying, trying to breathe. But I have to hold my breath and wait. Wait for the water to be still again. Then I can go back to being me but if my old self isn't there, I'll have to figure out who I am now. And I'm pretty sure Alastor killed the old me. So we will see who I become after all this. We will see the scars that he left me with. The ones that will be a reminder of him. But not going to lie I feel my reputation era coming on. It's coming soon. And you'll only know what that means if you know a little bit about T swift. But, even though I'm going to be in my reputation era, I still get anxious. Like right now, I'm anxious. Anxious because everything with my book is happening soon. The go fund me, advertising, and buying publishing services. It's coming very soon and kind of freaking me out. But I'm totally ready for all of it. I'm ready for everything after it too. I've planned, prepared, and planned some more for this. I know what I'm doing when I'm doing it, if it'll cost me anything. Everything. I'm ready for when it comes. But I'm scared. More so of the Social media aspect of it. Like posting on Instagram. I'm scared that all the judgmental teenagers will have something snotty to say. Make fun of me. I'm not scared of posting on Facebook. That's nothing. Grownups and old people don't scare me. If anything they should be scared of me. But it's *me* so they don't have to be. But I'm also thinking of being in school. I'll be in school and people will know I'm mentally Ill and wrote a book about it. That will be awkward. Embarrassing. Also the teachers will know. That will be weird. More uncomfortable than weird, but still. Gosh why can't I stop thinking?! Like just stop. Shut off. All the time. Just thoughts thoughts

thoughts thoughts thoughts. Like just be quiet for like 5 minutes. Please. Jesus Christ.

And I'm sorry, I haven't really been keeping you up to date with my job stuff. I have been wanting a job, but I haven't put any new resumes out. My dad's friend hooked me up with an interview at Esquire's. My dad had pretty good contacts I guess. I got an interview and it went well. And they pretty much hired me. I have paperwork to fill out and I will bring it, then they'll get me on the schedule. It doesn't seem like I truly have the job. Probably not till I get my schedule. But I'm going to be a hostess. And kind of a support person. Clean tables, get coffees, takeout orders, bring people to their tables, give 'em menus. That kind of thing. Pretty easy job, just gotta get into the other Crew worker's groove. I'm excited. It's a nice place, super nice people. Only 15 minutes away. Ooo also I forgot to tell you, we have a go fund me date. May 1st. I have pictures ready to post and everything. That's part of the reason I really wanted a job. In case the go fund me doesn't go well I need to make money. But I'm hoping I'll do well. I hope I'll only have to pay for editing, or maybe just buying the copies if I do really well. We will see.

I'm getting anxious though. But it's a mix of good and bad. I'm so excited, this is a big thing. It's exciting. But I am also terrified. Of the outcome. Makes me nervous. Putting my whole self out there. Giving everyone the perfect opportunity to bully me. Poke fun. But hey at least I'll be getting dough. Right? Everyone keeps telling me about how I'm gonna make the money back. And I could care less about that. I just want the book out there. And I'll do whatever I can to do that. I don't care about the profit, I should but I don't. I'm not into too much of the financial stuff. I like the business part. You know, the whole package. Having meetings about editing, cover design, formatting, layouts, stuff like that. I like that. But it's not distracting me enough. I'm feeling the bittersweet effects of this book soon being over. This book has saved me in a way. In a way that nothing else could have saved me. It will definitely be a grieving process I think. But hopefully the happiness of it being done, helping people. Out there. That'll make it better. I just love writing. It's something that's easy for me. Something I'm confident in. Something I can do that others can't. Don't get me wrong, everything doesn't instantly come to me. I need inspiration. Like music. Music is such a big part of my writing. All the music that makes my heart ache. That has a really big impact on my writing. I listen to lyrics and base a whole topic on that one word or saying. Also quotes. Quotes influence my writing too, just not near as much as music does. Music is so important to me. I love music so much. I wish I could listen to music any time I wanted. Like the times I want to escape from the dreadful real world. Times when I feel like everyone hates me. Thinks I'm annoying. I feel lately everyone has been finding me annoying. Anytime I'm trying to be positive or happy, or even excited about something. I'll tell someone and they give me the most 'I don't care attitude or response. Like god you're trying to make this hard for me aren't you? No wonder I find it so hard. No wonder I don't tell you my good news. I'm just tired of putting in effort into a relationship that's one sided. Or feels one sided. Or I hate it when I'm super confident and happy about something that I'm doing. And then they give me a doubtful reply. Or seem so uninterested and question all of it. Like sure thanks for putting a damper on my good mood. What the hell? I just don't understand people who do that kind of stuff but always get angry when other people do it to them. You're a hypocrite. That's literally what you are. Not you, not you who's reading this. Unless you do, do that, then yes *you* are a hypocrite. I refuse to feel buried by others. I refuse to make it *my* problem. They wanna act like that, go ahead. That's something that they need to work on with themselves. Makes me feel crazy. I know people are tired of me. Tired of my anxiety. They 'understand' I have anxiety, but get annoyed by me always overthinking, being nervous, and can't do all the things they can do easily. I know they talk about me to others. Saying stuff like that. I know. Or hey maybe I'm overthinking it, right? It's so obvious that they're getting irritated by it. Tired of having to 'deal' with it. Yeah because they are the ones dealing with it. Totally. Me and my anxiety come as a package deal. You choose me, you get my anxiety. If you don't want the anxiety I come with, then you don't get me. So instead of putting me through that, just drop me. Easy as that. I don't need to deal with this, it's bull. I've dealt with my mental health issues alone before, doesn't mean I can't do it again. And to be honest they don't contribute anything good to my mental health anyway. I have to do that myself. I really can do it all by myself. It feels lonely, but as of lately I've been feeling lonely anyways. I have no one to tell my good news to. No one I *want* to tell my good news to. And I understand if you're struggling with your mental health.

Alastor

Believe me I get it. But that doesn't give you any right to be rude to people. I struggle a lot and I'm not mean to anyone. Of course I can get irritated easily, and I *do* get irritated with others. But if it comes off rude, I apologize. It's not hard. Some people are just really self absorbed.

CHAPTER TWENTY FOUR
Destructive breakdown

Here I am the next day. Crying quietly to myself in the bathroom stall. Freaking out because I lashed out in class. I didn't realize what I was doing until I did it. My hands are shaking and my legs are wobbly. What the heck. Why can't I just stay quiet? What happened was I was in English and the teacher was poking fun at a kid and I was like yeah and mentioned something about it. Then someone said something like "shut up maya you're literally a toddler". They are not wrong but of course I reacted back by saying that he was an IPad kid. An iPad kid is one of those kids who sit funny and eat food while getting their IPad dirty. Then under my breath I said I hate this class. And my teacher said, "To sum all that up, Maya hates all of you". I think I went beat red. I realized what I had done. I talked back to someone, and put all the attention on me. After my teacher said that I hate everyone, someone in the back quietly said, "yeah and we all hate maya too". I pretended like I didn't hear anything. Class was over and I walked to my next class feeling like my legs were jello. I realized I couldn't stay in class so I asked if I could go to the washroom. That's when I first started to tell I was going to have a panic attack. I had to go back to class and I messaged my mom telling her what was going on. Texting her made it worse though. It was like I had to go through what happened all over again. I broke down. Felt like I couldn't breathe, I was shaking like crazy, crying, covering my face so people couldn't see. I sat like that for 15 minutes just texting my mom. Then of course those kids brought up the IPad kid thing again. And were like "right maya?" And I got up said "fucking Christ" and left the room sobbing. Which I hate. Because they think *they* made me cry. They didn't. I don't want them to think they have this power over me. Because they don't. Them talking to me was like my last straw. I bet you if I hadn't had the panic attack I would have tried to laugh it off with them, make light of the IPad kid situation. But I had a panic attack. And I wasn't having it. Didn't find it funny. I just wish they knew that I wasn't crying because of them, god. I don't want them to think I'm weak and pathetic. Because I'm not. Most of the time. After that I went to the washroom completely balling and Morgan came in to see if I was okay. Obviously I wasn't. But she tried to help me, and she gave me a hug. After that I called my mom. Again balling. And she told me my aunt was coming to get me. I had left my binder and thermos in class. Ugh. Had to go get it. I took a really big breath and walked, I was walking fast and in a determined way. My vision was blurry from the tears and the hall was full of grade 8s because it was their lunch. As soon as I walked in the room they went silent. I was thinking something along the lines of 'fuck I hate this'. I grabbed my stuff and told Morgan and Ella I was going home. Ila had left early that day. I walked out of the room and went straight upstairs to my locker. Grabbed my backpack and went to the office. I sat in the office waiting for my aunt and my mum called the receptionist. I heard her on the phone. I went up to the receptionist and said my name is Maya, I'm leaving. And she was like, "oh are you okay? You can wait right outside and your aunt will be here soon babe. Hope you feel better". She was really sweet. So I walked outside trying to breathe but feeling like I couldn't. And my aunt came and I left. God why does this always happen to me. I don't try to embarrass myself in front of the whole class. Like Jesus. It's honestly stupid how many times this has happens to me. At home I just keep thinking and thinking about it. Like can Alastor not? I already had to deal with it, now he wants me to think about it over and over? What the hell? That's the low of the low honestly. I'm getting knots in my stomach because he's making me relive it. I'm so tired too. I feel like I got hit by a bus. And my face isn't looking too good either. The bags under my eyes are atrocious and you can just tell I've been crying. I'm just so done. Absolutely done. Makes me think that thought again. Not being alive. Sounds pretty good right now. I'm just too tired. Too tired to deal with this. Life. Again I won't try anything I never would. I do want to live and be happy, but that's getting hard and taking too long to come. I'm just so tired. Too tired.

It's the next day. Of course I'm home. Trying to have a chill day. But last night I was so worked up about it so anxious that I almost vomited. I thought I was going to throw up so I had to stop eating my dinner. That's only happened a few times to me. Getting so worked up I'm nauseous. I can't believe it sometimes. How messed up I am. Why am I like this? Why? I'm so nervous to go back to school. I've been traumatized at school way too many times. And all those times, it was Alastors fault. Like fuck him. I'm over him and his crap. He ruins everything for me. Everything. I envy the people who don't worry like I do. I envy those you can get through a day of school without knots in their stomach or having a panic attack. Or those who don't need to see a counselor and a therapist. Those who don't need to take meds to help themselves. Even though they don't help me. Ugh. I'm just so angry and sick of it. I'm so sick of it. Just stop. Seriously, I feel like I'm going insane. Like I'm going to burst. Freak out. Loose my flippen marbles. I hate this. I hate that it's the night before I go back to school after what happened and my eyes are welling up and my stomach is turning, my hands are shaking, and I'm scared. Scared to go to school. I dread the looks I'm going to get. The feeling I'm going to have. Why can't this be over? All of it. My anxiety, Alastor, medication, *school*, the bags under my eyes, the losing weight, the shaking, the psychologist appointments. When will it be over? My heart is literally hurting. Carrying all this weight, this baggage. It feels like it's shutting down. My chest is tired. My heart just ran a marathon and is ready for bed now. But Alastor took the bed away. And stabbed my heart in the back. All me and my heart want is to be able to rest. Not worrying about the next day, not dreading it. Instead, being excited about it. We are exhausted. We can never catch a break. We thought the marathon we were running would have an end, until we found out we were running on a treadmill. A treadmill with no way to stop it or get off of it. Caged in a prison cell. Just going on and on. We've been running for a long time. When will Alastor let go? Turn it off. Give me a break. Will he ever? Who knows.

It's Friday now. I didn't go to school again. Which will be better I think, going back Monday. Give me and my class the weekend to forget about it. Tonight we celebrated Ella's birthday. We went bowling and brought some pizza there. It was really fun. Ella had a good time which is good. She liked her gifts. I tried an energy drink for the first time. Did absolutely nothing. My tiredness is undefeatable. Invincible. Nothing can make me not tired. Nothing. Because it's 11:16 and I'm ready to sleep. I'm exhausted. I'm just glad Ella had fun. We all had fun. We have a good friend group. Tomorrow I'm excited to do a little bit of everything and a little bit of nothing. Chores, laundry, deep cleaning, changing my

Alastor

bedding. My usual Sunday tasks, but on a Saturday. Livin on the edge aren't I. So crazy, so spontaneous. Anyways, I haven't had one of those days in a while. It'll be nice. Just watch criminal minds while doing chores. Sounds like a dream.

It's Sunday, the first of May. I posted my go fund me. My nerves were through the roof. I'm not sure why exactly because the excitement was kind of battling the nerves. But I'm at $400 dollars right now. I'm shocked at how generous some people are. Giving me $100 dollars. That's so nice. I'm beyond grateful. But obviously, since this book is about a fight against alastor. He wants nothing to do with it. He wants to make me worry about the go fund me. I was shaking as my mum posted it, shaking as I posted it. Still freaking out now. Almost an hour & half later. He's whispering in my ear as I'm trying to get my mind off it. "What if you're not going to make enough?" "You probably won't" "haha no one is reposting it" "that's sad" "this is pathetic, your pathetic" "this isn't going to go anywhere, your not going anywhere with this" I can't stop it. I can't stop him. He won't shut up. I don't know how any of this works. I don't know if $400 is good for it only being up for an hour. Is it? Alastor tells me no. He says that's horrible. Also why isn't anyone sharing it? I've seen them share things other people do, why not mine? Is it beicaise it's me? Oh it's Maya, don't share it if it's maya. Because she's not cool according to the social standards of middle schoolers. It just doesn't seem fair. It's not fair to me. Some people I thought I was somewhat friends with, dont care? They don't even care enough to press 2 buttons to share it? Don't get me wrong I'm *beyond* grateful for what I have right now and the people who are sharing it. But I expected some "friends" to share it. Not Ella, Ila, Morgan, or Charlotte. It would be nice of them. But it's the other people. Anyways. I am just so excited, scared, and grateful all balled up into one. I don't know how I'm going to sleep tonight. Or function for the rest of the day. I literally do not know what to do with myself. Everyone is telling me I'm doing amazing, that they're so proud, that I should be proud. And I want to, I feel proud, but I'm not enjoying it. Because of Al.

It's the same day. 9:02pm, way past my bedtime I know. I'm at $880 right now. Just wow. I'm amazed at the generosity. I'm so thankful. Anyways, to steer away from that, I will keep you updated though. I got my shifts for my new job. Which is exciting. Everyone there is super nice and seems to actually train their new staff. Which is also a good thing. I feel like this job will be good for me. I'll be working short shifts to start, and probably till the end of the school year. But once summer starts I'll be able to work 8 hour shifts which is what I want. I think that it'll be a better work environment for me. I'm getting really tired now, so it's time to log off now. I'll probably talk to you tomorrow. Goodnight.

It's the next day. I was going to go to school. I mentally prepared myself. But my mum needed me home to help her with stuff. She's not feeling the best. I've raised $935 dollars. Wow. It's only been one day. I'm so thankful.

Lol. It's Wednesday now. I'm at $1400. I can't believe it. I'm shocked. Like I can buy a cellphone and a chrome book with that. That's insane. I'm 350 dollars away from being halfway. And 2100 from being done. It's just completely insane. Again, I'm just so grateful. Now at 1600. This is insane.

I start my new job today. I'm excited. I think it will be good. I just wish I could drive. I feel bad for my parents all the time, driving me to and from work. I want a beetle which I think

I've said before, then a Jeep for my grown up car. Can't wait to go to McDonald's by myself. Order Pepsi, fries, & ice cream. I'll probably go to a dollar store or sobeys or something and buy random crap I don't need but just want. And as I'm doing this I'll drive there blasting Ms T swift. And go home blasting Ms T swift. I know I will scream while singing it. This gives me summer vibes. Something I'll do the summer after next. Just on a random night I don't have plans. I'm excited for summer. More so because school will be over and I'll be leaving the hell hole school I go to now. All the teachers are talking about how school is ending soon. Wrap up tests coming up and stuff like that. Little scary because I don't like tests in the subjects we're doing but I'll deal. I know I will be sad at the end of the year. Because I won't be able to see Ms C or Ms G every week. I won't be able to slack off and miss school when I want. Things just won't be the same. I won't have my friends with me all day. It will just be different. I'm in no way going to miss school, this school in particular. Wish I could flip off everyone I hate there. Everything is going to change a lot though. My brother will be moving out by the end of summer. That's crazy to me. He won't be there. It makes me kind of sad. But to be honest I don't see him very often anyways. Then I'll be going to highschool. He will be going to college. Big things are happening. But like I've said before, I know this summer is going to be good. I just got a feeling.

I worked at my new job. It was hard the first day, but good, way better the second day. I loved it. The job itself is pretty self explanatory. It's just getting faster at it, getting the groove of it. Everyone there is so nice. You can tell they are like a family. It's sweet. They are all very approachable & helpful. I'm glad I'm working there. This job will be good for me.

I have written in a while. 'A while' being less than a week. But I was thinking about what I just wrote. I really thought I knew myself so well. Well enough to know I don't need to hurt myself. But I'm shocked. Shocked at what I just did. I was lighting a candle. But as I stated at the match, the fire was starting to go away. I lit the candle. I took my hand, put them in fists and held it above the flame. The pain scared me at first. Made me flinch. But then I got used to it. It's now a little bit red with yellow in the center. I did the rest of my right hand, because I'm left handed. You can see marks only on three fingers on my right hand, the one yellowish red one, a red and pink circle one of my ring finger, and a tiny light red on my pointer finger. I did my left hand too. It was harder because I'm not used to using my right hand. On my left hand there are also only three noticeable marks. They all are just reddish and pink on this hand. With little circles of where the skin is burned. I never would have thought I'd do this. I was capable of doing this. I always thought I was too scared. Because of Alastor. But he was taunting me in a way this time. "You're too big of a baby to do it" "You're not brave enough, not strong enough". I wanted to prove him wrong. And I did. But why did I do it? Do I deserve it? I don't know. I'm shaking right now. Trembling. I'm in shock about what I did. Everything has been so overwhelming lately. Crazy. Really busy. Started a new job, babysitting on top of that, drama I could care less about, appointments on top of appointments. Either about my meds, my book, braces, anything. And it's not even two weeks into may yet. I'm busy trying to schedule everything on top of school and work. But school seems like the least of my concerns. I'm home today. I just couldn't get up. I couldn't. I didn't and don't care. My eyes are filling up with tears. I burned myself? And it wasn't an accident. I did it on purpose. On purpose without even realizing. I wasn't thinking. my mind was blank. But yet it wasn't. I want to tell my mom. But what will she think? What will people think? What if people notice, what will I say?

I told my mum. Bad idea. I don't know if she was angry. But it seemed like it. She didn't know what to do. She thought it was me just doing it just for fun or an accident. But I don't know what it was. She seemed so angry. I just wanted help. I freaked myself out. I wasn't thinking. This is by far one of the worst panic attacks I've ever had. My whole entire body is vibrating. Whole body is shaking. And I can't stop myself from it. I can't calm myself down. My breathing is uncontrollable, just like the shaking. And the tears are just falling like crazy. A waterfall out of my eyes. I don't know what to do. What do I do with myself? They're not going to check me into a mental hospital. They're not going to send me to a hospital. I don't even think the burn classifies as a 1st degree burn. I feel like I have a fever. This is how I shake when I have a fever. It's like I'm cold when I'm not, I think I'm cold so I lay on the side of my bed where the heater is. And the heat feels good. My whole body is also stinging. In a prickly way it started just with my face. My face was stinging then it led to my whole body.

I messaged my brother, Samantha, and Morgan. I didn't know who else to talk to. My brother didn't understand I don't think. But he was just telling me to breathe and chill out. Morgan was really concerned about me. Just wanted me to be okay. I felt bad afterwards about telling her. Making her worry. Samantha just asked where I was, I told her I was at home. That I didn't go to school today. But she hasn't responded. She read it but didn't respond. So assuming she's just working, too busy to talk. Which is understandable. She's probably working with kids who are going through way worse than me. But I was her advice. Help from her. Tell me what I should do. Maybe she can tell me what I was thinking because I have no clue what I was thinking. I'm looking at the marks on my knuckles in pure shock and guilt. Why? What did I do that for? I genuinely don't know. I want someone to tell me. Figure this out for me. Tell me what's going on because I have no clue. Someone who will understand. I don't want to be home right now. I want to leave but I have nowhere to go. I might just go to the park. No one will be there in the middle of the day. It's not bad weather. I could just go, take a breather. Mostly. I just want to hear what Samantha has to say. She's really the only one who can help me. This is one of those times when I wish I could drive. Drive somewhere random. Where people won't know where I am. A place where no one will be there. I can be alone. Walking 5 minutes to park isn't enough. And I can't call someone like my aunt or nan to pick me up. They'd want to talk about it. It would be cool if my brother had his license. I'd ask him to come home to pick me up. And he'd just drive, he wouldn't ask any questions. He'd probably just blast his music and drive. That would be really nice right about now. I just want to leave. Not be here right now. Part of me is wishing that Samantha or my brother would just show up at the house. Pick me up and drive me around. But I know they both can't do that. Especially Samantha. I feel bad for disturbing her work day.

It's a bit later. And I think I'm realizing why I did what I did. Well not a reason yet. But it was an impulse. I wasn't thinking about anything. I just did it. Why? Couldn't tell you. It was crazy, I just impulsively did it. I didn't want to hurt or harm myself. I didn't want to set myself on fire, or do it for fun. I just did it. I want to know why but I don't. After I did it, I spiraled into a panic attack. A really bad one. That's all I know so far. But I hope as I de-stress a bit it will be more clear.

I stayed home again. I know, I know. 'You need to go to school Maya' I can hear you saying it. Thinking it. I'm just waiting for this earth to not be so scary. A place where I can be happy. Not a place I wish would swallow me whole. Why am I like this? What brainy chemicals make my mind work like this? Why don't meds work? Why does no one around me understand? Or relate, even just a little. I have a heavy weight on my chest. A tragically painful weight. Not hollow, not empty. A dense feeling, one you can't lift up, remove, make lighter. Permanent. Fucking Christ I'm so done with this. Dealing with it. I want this to be gone. Like if Alastor fell off a cliff, no one would miss him. I'm waiting. And I am and have been waiting patiently. Missing the feeling of how I am when I'm laughing so hard and loud. A real pure laugh. The smiles I get aren't fake. The proudness I feel when I accomplish something. I'll continue to wait, wait until all the bad days don't last months. Wait till all the good days don't last moments. They last longer. Wait for the happiness to not be temporary.

CHAPTER TWENTY FIVE
The end

Today will be a good day? I like my outfit a lot. I got a decent lunch for school. My classes aren't too bad today. It's nice out today. I'm going to see Dr Strange Multiverse of Madness. A new marvel movie. I'm going to see it with my mum, my aunt, and Morgan. I'm excited for that. Movie theater food is amazing. It will be a good day right? Seems like it. I hope it is. It's Friday the 13th, May 2022. Friday the 13th. I don't know if I believe in that stuff. But normally bad things happen on Friday the 13th. A lil bit spooky. We will see what the day has to bring.

Also, this is the last chapter. I'm shocked. Sad and happy. More proud than happy. We've come so far. Far might not be the best but we still got here. Got to this point. I'm feeling more sad than proud right now. But that's okay. All good things must come to an end.

I wrote that on the bus this morning. I'm on the bus home now. So today has been good so far. My outfit was comfortable, and I felt semi confident. It was hot today though so that wasn't the best. We barely did anything in class all day. If we did something it was easy. Little funny things happened. So I laughed for little reasons. And felt genuinely happy for a little bit of time. Which is good. I'm as happy as I can get for now. My friends obviously were the ones I was laughing with. My food was good. I bought iced tea today, I thought it wouldn't be good because I had no lemons to add in. But it actually tasted really good. It was a perfect day to bring it. Because it was hot and all. I'm excited for the movie tonight. Morgan's coming just short of 2 hours early to hang and have time to get dollar store candy so we don't have to buy the overpriced movie candy. Also going early to give us time to play around in the arcade. But before we leave to do that stuff I'm going to show her my ideas for the cover of this book. Because Morgan is a really good drawer, I'm going to get her to draw my idea and I'm going to send in her drawing to the cover designer. That way they get the complete idea in a good drawing. Not a bad one like I did it. I'm not artistically talented. Anyways, I'm excited. I think the cover perfectly matches. I feel like it suits the book. Represents the way feelings look on the outside.

Also, something I forgot to tell you is that they upped my meds. Again. I'm at the highest dose of sertraline. 200 mg of that and 1 mg of Ablify or whatever. They said if nothing changes in 2 weeks, then you know it really doesn't work for me. It's been one week, and it looks like it doesn't work for me. But one thing that doesn't make sense to me is that my meds are anti depressants. Not anti anxiety, well not your typical anti anxiety meds. So I'm curious as to why I'm on these and not something more suited for anxiousness.

Yesterday was Saturday. My dad and I went to the mall. It was so nice outside. It was warm, but not too hot where it's dreadful. It was the perfect temperature with the perfect amount of wind. On the drive to the mall we listened to Olivia Rodrigo. My dad and I both love her music. I played Déjà vu, good for you, happier, and jealousy jealousy. Jealousy jealousy is both of our favorites. The windows were rolled down. The wind was in my hair. Not too crazy though because I had a hat on. And the sun was shining. I was singing the songs. It felt like summer. It was awesome. I was wearing Jean shorts and this mocha coloured tank top, with my white low top converse and my green Tommy Hilfiger hat. It showed me how much I really do love summer. How fun it can be. It was awesome. Going to the mall was a pretty easy trip too. I got a white button up top that I'm in love with. A cool colorful tank top, sunglasses, and jeans. Blue jeans with no rips. Because I needed a pair with no rips. Everything was pretty easy to find. And I didn't overspend. That's something I'm trying to work on. I only overspent by like 20 bucks. That's not bad. After we got home from the mall, I did some chores and bummed around. Then I went to work. I wasn't too excited about going to work. I was nervous. It was my last training shift and I thought I might suck or forget everything or not be good enough so they would be mad at me. But I went and it was actually pretty good. I did everything well. I did need help with takeout orders and I'm not the fastest but they say that takeout is hard and it's okay, I just haven't gotten my rhythm yet. Everyone there is so nice. Makes it comforting. And I feel like I'm always going to be nervous to go in or not want to work, but when I actually *go in* and *work* I love it. It's fun, easy. I also think that I feel better because I made amazing tips. I got $50 bucks worth of tips. Which is insane. I was shocked. Today, I did the rest of my chores. I'm going to get my nails done by one of the littles moms, that's her job. Nails, waxing, eyebrows, face stuff. Those kinds of things. And not long after I'll be going to work, come home, shower, go to bed. May has been so busy for me. So busy. Like I'm too busy. I'm tired. I can handle it but I'm just worn out. I think that this should be my last week of craziness, the next week will mostly just be a random appointment or two and work. I don't mind that. I don't know why everything was so jammed packed into the first two weeks of May though. If I had control over it all, it would all be spread across the month of may. Anyways, I'm hungry so I'm going to go eat breakfast. Talk to ya later.

Same day. But now it's 8:38pm. Today was good but hectic. Did chores, went to get my nails done, did more chores, went to work, came home and did a few little things. Showered. Now I'm in bed writing to you. I'm really happy with how things are going with work. I love it there. Like I actually love my job. It's good. And the people are so nice. Everything is going well there. I made more tips, and was told that I'm doing amazing. So obviously that makes me feel better. But right now I feel good. I'm all nice and clean from my shower. My room is all nice and clean. I have fresh bedding on with shaven legs so that feels good. And even though today was a bit crazy, it was a good day. I'm also probably just a little happy that I'm not going to school tomorrow. I have a braces appointment tomorrow morning and I'm assuming my mouth will be sore so I'll be home for the day. So I get to sleep in a little, and be a bum for the rest of the day after a crazy long week and weekend. I have one more crazy week to get through until things start to chill out again. And I'm really looking forward to the chilling. Also something that's been on my mind recently is graduation. My middle school graduation. And the prom I have. I have a really pretty burgundy dress and I'm buying some charcoal coloured converse. I might get my nails done too. Probably a sage color. I feel like it might be fun. But also scary. Very scary. Or maybe less scary, more weird and uncomfortable. Who knows. We will see. I just can't wait to get out of this hellhole of school. It will not be a bittersweet goodbye. I'm not going to miss it. Of course I'll miss Ms C and Ms G but that's all. There are 31 days left of school. 1 month's worth, not including weekends. I can't

Alastor

believe it. It went so slow yet so fast. I'm just so excited for summer. The big things come if you are exams, grad, and prom. All in June. So the rest of May is just regular work and prep for exams, then we move on to the bigger stuff. But I feel like these last 31 days will fly by. Let's hope that they don't. Just so I can try to enjoy my last weeks at school before summer. Hope they aren't too hard on me. Lately I've been slacking off and super unmotivated, so I'm behind on my work. But it's also occurring to me that exactly 159 days & 22 ½ weeks ago I started writing to you. I've taken you through 5 months and a week of my life. I will not be taking you through summer, but it's not that interesting anyways. This year has been my most eventful one yet. Not entirely in a good way. There's been lots of tears. Which is why I'm so grateful that I've had you to talk to, my friends and family, & two amazing teachers to help me get through the school year. 30 days left of the school year and I'll bet you I'll show up for 15 of them. I've in total missed 540 classes, and 100 days of school. New record beat.

This year has been filled with ups and downs. Many big downs but a couple of good ups. Looking back at myself a year ago, I was a completely different person. Same with 2 years ago, and 2 years before that. All different people. But the same Maya. I often think of baby me. Baby Maya. So sweet, sassy, carefree, didn't have a worry in the world. I miss her. I wish I could hug her. Or even hug a 10 year old me. Just tell me to never grow up, but if you have to. Don't worry. Everything happens for a reason, reasons you may not like. But you'll be okay. Everything will work out. Enjoy every little thing, enjoy the stupid things that make you laugh even when your sad. Always live in the moment, learn to not hold a grudge, not only on others, but yourself too. Be careful & be kind. But do not feel the need to hold back, you'll never know the outcome of things you never said. Of course they might not all be good outcomes, but necessary ones. You're brave, so stay like that. You're smart too, don't let anyone make you feel differently. You are built for success, so don't rain down on all of your ideas. Take care of yourself. It's okay to have your rough days. It's okay to eat junk and be lazy. It's okay to not want to go out or go to school. It's okay to not be perfect or look perfect, because no one's perfect. It's okay, just take care of yourself. Don't lose your special smile. Be you. Yourself. Kind of sounds cheesy but it's true. Being yourself is the best you can be. Love yourself too. You deserve it. Focus on only what YOU can control. Don't drive yourself crazy. That's everything I wish I could say to my little self. Warn her. But it's also a reminder to me and you *now*. To be happy.

I'm starting a new chapter in my life in about 108 days give or take. It's a big chapter of my life. High school. It's daunting. I'm completely terrified but also so ready for the change. This is a change I've been waiting for and I think I'm ready for. Obviously it's a new thing and I'm terrified but it will be good. Different. I'm going to have to learn to be a little more social, see if I can make new friends. I'm not going to push myself though. Baby steps. It will be something I adapt to. Longer classes, big school, new teachers, new students, different class subjects. It will be so different. I think the only 2 things that will be the same are my backpack and my anxiety. Maybe I'll find a little bit of comfort in those. I will not however find comfort in Alastor. Anxiety is normal. My anxiety levels are too high, which is what alastor is. An excessive amount of anxiety and really bad mindset and thinking. That's what he is. I don't even know if I refer to him as a he anymore. He doesn't deserve that. Alastor is an 'it'. That's all Alastor is.

Alastor is still just as ruthless and a bully as usual. Nothing changed in that respect. I often find myself having too much to say, or writing just so much, it's never ending. But as I'm trying to finish this chapter, this book. I'm at a loss of words. I don't know what to say. This book is my rock, my favorite thing I've ever done, and I don't know what to say. Mental health is a pain in the ass. That's something to say. It goes up and down and never leaves you steady. It's what I imagine surfing is like. Just have to learn to balance. And you balance until the big wave comes and crashes into you. You think you're drowning. Until the water calms down again and you can float, just keep your head above water. I don't want you to drown. Keep pushing to get to the sandy sunny beach that we will all arrive at once the storm ends. I see the beach as happiness. And the stormy waters as Alastor. And I know you're trying because I am too, I know what it's like. Feels like no one understands or notices how bad it's getting. But I guess I just want to tell you you're doing great. You're doing amazing. I know you're just surviving, barely getting by. But that's okay. Do what you have to do to get to the bright days. The moments that make life worth living. Live for those little things. Don't wait for them, just let them happen. These are also things I want to remind myself to think of. The good days won't come if I wait for them. I also get to think of how we are tiny little meaningless humans, the size of a crum. On this huge floating ball in space. Space. Nothing matters if you think of it in that way. That stuff is mind boggling to me. Who gives a flying fudge if you wear that outfit, go to school or not, embarrass yourself, are sad, angry, or literally anything. We are on a flipping floating ball in this big black space. And I know, I know. You don't think of that at the moment those bad things are happening. Or just because that's true doesn't mean it doesn't still hurt, or affect you, I know. But still isn't it fun to think of? Like enjoy everything you want to, do everything that you in your power, can do. Who cares about other people's opinions. They won't matter in a month, year, decade. So don't dwell on it. Enjoy the sunrises and sunsets. Or the feeling of laughing so hard your stomach hurts. The excitement of getting coffee. End of school feeling. The smell of new candles. The feeling of accomplishment. Enjoy everything, enjoy it all. But do it for you. Yourself. Do what will make you happy in the end. I know that I want to be successful, independent, and love my career. I want my cute little dream house with a dog and a cat. I want to be able to go out for coffee every weekend. Hangout with friends, but still have my alone time. I want to treat myself often, by buying little things like flowers for myself. I want to have a boyfriend in the future who doesn't want kids, and doesn't care about marriage. Also me being rich wouldn't be bad. I want to be very smart financially but also be able to buy things anytime I want. But most of all, I want my life to be filled with spontaneity. No day that feels the same. Something new and different every morning I wake up. That's what I want.

And I do feel a bit like a hypocrite because I always dwell on things like that and always overthink. But I want to be more carefree. A live in the moment type. That's a new goal of mine.

I've taken you guys for almost a full circle of my year. School year at least. Well actually half, but whatever. Felt like longer. Anyways I just want to say thanks. For always being here for me to talk too. It's been a big help. Because I'm here. I've done this. I can't quite say I've made it yet, but I did do this.

And I think after all this all I have to say is that I hate him. And I hate him for what he's done to me, but I will continue to put up with it until I don't have to. I'm determined and I think that's enough. He is pathetic & there's something I've been trying to refrain from saying. But I think I deserve you to say it. Fuck you Alastor. And I'm saying that with the biggest, pettiest smile.

I don't care how crazy I might sound. Talking about the person in my head. I'm not insane, it just makes it easier. Almost acting like a kid again. Making things up to make yourself feel better.

I am going to try to let go, ease up a bit. I know it'll be hard. But I want to forgive myself, not beat myself up. I want to find out who I am without my anxiety. I also feel like I'm going to have a hard time letting go of this. This book. It's all that I've had to use to fight against It. My only weapon. It'll be hard for me to get a new one and sad to see this go. But it makes me so happy to think that people will read this and hopefully feel better. Make them feel less alone. Or just relate to the feeling. That was the main goal here. And I'm so happy and excited to see this crazy idea of mine actually come to life. Be real. I'm definitely feeling mixed emotions. Sad that it will be gone. Happy it will help people. And proud that it's done, I did it. I hope that the next time I talk to you I'm doing better, and I can tell you all the good things that you'd want to hear. But We'll see. I'm also hoping that I won't be any worse. I hope that I'll be able to manage Alastor better or start to slowly wean him out of my head. I know the reason I have anxiety is a chemical imbalance in my brain, but that's really not what it feels like. It feels personal in a way, like He's out to get me. And this whole book might be crap. But I really do not care. I want this book to be whatever you want it to be. It can be your comfort book, your favorite book, least favorite book, I'd hope not but it can be if it is. I want this book to be your friend. I can be your friend. This book can be helpful to parents to see what it's like to be a teenager. A look into a kid's mental health and struggles. I want this book to always be something to come back to when you're feeling alone.

And I know you guys won't experience the end of school with me, exams, grad. All that stuff. But let's be honest, I write the best when I'm sad, and we all know I will not be sad about that. It will be a stressful, anxious filled month with a lot of relief and laughs. So not to worry you won't be missing much.

Monday, May 16th, 2022: This isn't a self help book, at all. Because to be honest, I don't have much to give. No amazing advice. But if i can suggest something, it is to not blame yourself. You have, in no way, caused any of it. And this book does not have a perfect ending. I'm not magically happy, because that's not how it works. This book is real. True to what I wanted it to be. This is a truthful experience of mine, and how nothing has gotten rid of the monster that lives in my head. That's what it is. It's just a monster. Just don't let them beat you. Alastor has before. Many times. But I'm still here. Not going to lie, I might be a little wobbly, but I'm still going. I will not let him win. Because I don't deserve that. So don't let your mind win. I want you to feel the relief and the success in not losing to your thoughts. I want that for me too. And this might not work for everyone, but giving that thing in your head a name. makes it easier to not blame it on yourself. Someone to be mad at. It helped me. He is still there obviously but it's nice to know that it's him doing all this. It's his fault. Samantha showed me that. I also want you to have hope, hold on to the hope. Even when it feels like you shouldn't. You deserve the world. Because you are strong. Stronger than you'll ever know. Battling your own mind is such a hard thing. Don't let anyone tell you otherwise. Just keep going, because you will be okay. And I will be okay too. Life moves on, so don't stop growing.

My heart hurts writing this. I didn't think it would be this hard to let go. I am proud. I'm so proud of myself. And of you. I did this. We did this. As I write these last pages to you tears are filling my eyes. I don't know if they are happy tears or sad ones. Maybe both. My heart is aching. What will I have to go to? Where will I vent when I don't have this anymore? This has helped fill the void feeling I've had. Will I feel empty when this is over? I need to be able to write. But I can't keep this to myself. I've worked too hard to not share this. Maybe I'll write another one for you, one in highschool. Sounds easy enough.

There's definitely no perfect way to end this, but I think I did an okay job. To be honest it's not really resonating with me that this is over. I'm in shock, disbelief. I'm going to come back to this. Add my finishing touches. And then it will be done. I can't believe I'm saying that. It's done. Wow. Thanks for growing up with me.

It's Wednesday June 8th 2022, and as sad as it makes me to say this, I have to. This book is coming to its end and I shouldn't prolong it.

Thanks again.

And until next time,

-Maya

CREDITS & THANK YOU'S

My parents Shelly and Bunty Soni should take credit for dealing with me. Always yapping about my book. But also for the huge amount of support, encouragement, and help they've given me.

My Aunt, Kim. She should take a lot of credit not just for the smoothness of the work we've done, but the whole process of it all. Even though she doesn't know much about writing or publishing, she continued to guide me through it. She spent so much time working on it and I'm beyond grateful.

Kelsey Murphy, another big thank you goes out to you. You took time out of your days to work on my book. Your help goes a long way. Thank you for your time & support.

And another thank you to all of the friends and family that have helped with the book itself, helped me get to this point, or we're just rooting for me. Thank you.

Manufactured by Amazon.ca
Bolton, ON